THE JOY WITHIN

Joan Goldstein
and Manuela Soares

THE JOY WITHIN
A Beginner's Guide
to Meditation

**PRENTICE
HALL
PRESS**

New York London Toronto Sydney Tokyo Singapore

Mandala from *Mandala* by Jose and Miriam Arguelles,
Copyright © 1972. Reprinted by arrangement with Shambhala Publications, Inc.

Lotus figure by Joan Goldstein.

PRENTICE HALL PRESS
15 Columbus Circle
New York, NY 10023

PRENTICE HALL PRESS and colophons are registered trademarks
of Simon & Schuster, Inc.

Library of Congress Cataloging-in-Publication Data

Goldstein, Joan.
The joy within : a beginner's guide to meditation /
by Joan Goldstein and Manuela Soares.
    p.   cm.
Includes bibliographical references.
ISBN 0-13-511338-5
1. Meditation.   I. Soares, Manuela.   II. Title.
BF637.M4G64   1990
158'.12—dc20   90-32759
                                                  CIP

Designed by Victoria Hartman

Manufactured in the United States of America

Dedicated to our beloved Gurumayi,
whose compassion and grace
made this book possible.

Contents

Preface

BY JOAN GOLDSTEIN

I discovered meditation while I was the editor of *Modern Screen* and *Movie Mirror*—two great chronicles of celebrity gossip. My mind was frenzied with having to have an inside track on what the stars were doing and with whom, constant deadlines, brainstorming for new ideas, and trying to keep ahead of the competition in newsstand sales.

It was during this very busy and often chaotic time that I was first introduced to meditation through Silva Mind Control, which promised rest and relaxation, the power to heal, and the power to control one's own mind, all of which I decided I needed. Through guided meditations, I learned, at will, to go into the alpha level of consciousness, which is the level of universal vibration and light meditation. I learned that our brain waves reveal four levels of consciousness. The beta level is the one in which we function during the waking state. Alpha is the level of refreshment and renewal and occurs not only during meditation, but every time we blink our eyes and daydream. Theta is the level of deep meditation, and delta is the deep sleep state.

Those of us who took the course discovered that we actually felt high from our alpha meditations. We were relaxed, extremely happy, and even giddy. In addition to this, we were able to function at a highly psychic level. For me the greatest benefit of meditation was the inner peace and happiness I began to experience. Instead of driving myself crazy trying to come up with ideas for coverlines each month, I would just go into an alpha meditation and the ideas would come up by themselves. When I felt burned out at the end of the day, I would quickly revive myself with a twenty minute alpha nap.

A few years later, an article in *New York* magazine caught my eye. It was about Swami Muktananda, an Indian master of meditation who could give people the experience of being bathed in love merely by brushing them with a wand of peacock feathers.

Up until this point, love had always been both my ecstasy and agony. It was a peak experience when it was all new and romantic, but that phase seemed to have a cap of six months to a year. After this so-called honeymoon period, personality conflicts would begin to surface and over the course of the next few years, the agony would slowly begin to outweigh the ecstasy and eventually the relationship would end, leaving me in such deep pain it was hard for me to believe I would ever survive it. Each time a relationship ended it felt as though I had lost a part of me I could never replace.

So the experience of being bathed in love simply by being brushed with a wand of feathers was something that appealed to me. But as much as I wanted to experience this otherworldly phenomenon taking place in New York's famed Catskill Mountains, I found excuses not to pursue it.

It wasn't until two years later that I felt a deep longing in my heart. I didn't know what that longing was for, but it was there. On the outside things looked great. I was still busy churning out movie magazines, partying with the stars, and living with a man who was a fellow adventurer. But in the middle of all this, there was still something missing.

A friend of mine had mentioned that she was studying

yoga. As far as I was concerned, nothing could be more boring. A hatha yoga class preceded one of the modern dance classes I took and I wondered what on earth people could possibly get from such slow, almost imperceptable movement. For me exercise had to be dynamic. It had to burst with energy and cover space; be filled with leaps, lunges, and turns. But one day, she invited me to an introductory meditation program held where she had been studying yoga. When I asked her to tell me more about it, she mentioned Swami Muktananda. I remembered his name. I remembered the article I had read. I remembered feeling like I had lost a once-in-a-lifetime opportunity by not going to meet him. Now, I was being given the chance to go to an introductory program in one of his ashrams. I didn't care that he was in India; I didn't care what the program was about. All I knew was that I had to go.

That was in 1978. The minute I walked through the doors of the ashram, I knew I had come home. It wasn't until about nine months later that I actually met Muktananda, or Baba, as he was known to his devotees.

If walking into the ashram in Manhattan was like coming home, meeting Baba and being blessed with his wand of peacock feathers showed me that home was actually in my own heart. Wave after wave of love washed over me as tears of joy streamed down my cheeks. At the same time, I felt as though I were flying. The longing I had felt in my heart was replaced by unconditional love. The lack I had been feeling was filled, but from within myself, through the grace of Baba Muktananda. As I continued to practice meditation, that inner reservoir of joy began to spill over into my daily life. In 1982, Baba transferred the power of his lineage of great masters to Gurumayi Chidvilasananda, and six months later he left his body.

Today Gurumayi continues to awaken love and the power of meditation inside everyone who meets her. Being with her has totally transformed my life, and the way I see life. I come from a place of calmness instead of frenzy; peace instead of angst; love instead of fear. Under Gurumayi's guidance, I no longer have to go off in search of adventure. Every moment has become an adventure, because every moment is an opportunity for growth and expansion.

When we turn within there's unlimited treasure waiting to be explored, unlimited resources from which we can draw for our own enrichment and joy.

It is my hope that this book will be the first leg of a long and exciting journey within for all of you who have come this far.

Preface

BY MANUELA SOARES

In 1980, while working at a fast-paced, high-pressure job, a
friend invited me to visit Swami Muktananda at his ashram
in South Fallsburg, New York. She spoke glowingly about
meditation and the joy she experienced in Muktananda's
presence. Intrigued by her radiance, and looking for better
ways to cope with the stresses and strains of my job, I went
to meet Muktananda.

This was the first time I had ever tried meditation, but in
Muktananda's presence I experienced a tremendous sense of
calm and peace. My mind wasn't a constant blur of thoughts.
This was remarkable for someone who was always on the
go and had never been able to sit still for more than five
minutes at a time. The most extraordinary thing that happened was that I went without a cigarette for three days. A
three-pack-a-day smoker, I'd never gone more than a day
without one.

Each evening it was customary for ashram guests to greet
Muktananda with flowers or fruit. During one of his evening talks, he suggested that we could give him anything
we wanted to be freed of—alcohol, cigarettes, or any negative behaviors or emotions. As I went up to say good-bye
to Baba on the last night, I silently offered him my smoking
habit. As I drove away from South Fallsburg, I threw away

my last pack of Marlboro Lights, and with it, my addiction to nicotine.

The more I meditated, the more I began to experience life as a flow of events. Instead of doing my utmost to control whatever was happening, meditation helped me to deal more calmly and joyfully with whatever life presented. As a result, my anxiety level decreased considerably, and I was a lot less frustrated when things didn't go my way. Now when things go wrong, I'm not only able to cope, but I'm also able to enjoy the other things that are right with my life. And when things are going well, meditation lets me experience that happiness as my own inner state.

A few years ago, I went through a difficult period when everything seemed to fall apart—someone very close to me died, I lost a new job, and it looked like I would have to find a new apartment. One thing after another continued to go wrong, but I managed to keep my equilibrium and even a sense of humor. During these crises, a friend remarked, "I really admire how you've handled all the things that have happened. I would have been a wreck, but you're down-right cheerful." Her comment took me by surprise. For a moment, I didn't understand what she meant. What other way was there to respond to all of the outer turmoil? It wasn't that my problems didn't exist, they just didn't over-whelm me the way they might have a few years earlier.

On a recent meditation retreat, I met a woman from Scotland who had only recently begun to meditate. When she learned that I was working on a book about how to meditate, she looked at me in surprise. "Goodness," she exclaimed, "I'll bet that's a short book!"

It made me laugh because, in truth, meditation *is* very simple. With a few words of explanation, anyone can learn to meditate. All you need is your own self and a quiet place. That's what's so wonderful about meditation, you can take it anywhere and do it anytime; it doesn't require any special equipment. And yet, for such a simple exercise, it is so complex that for centuries people have devoted their entire lives to its study and practice.

Meditation is very simple, yet it is filled with subtlety. It can reveal a whole new inner landscape that you hadn't ever considered before. It's like discovering that your house or apartment has more rooms than you thought it did. This book is meant to help you explore all of that extra space, to discover the geography of your inner landscape.

Meditation is like a flower. With a little care, some sun and water, and time, the bud unfolds into a beautiful blossom. In the same way, when we meditate regularly in a quiet place, in time, the inner self unfolds in all its beauty and reveals the joy that lies within.

THE JOY WITHIN

Introduction

A sign in a window reads, "Joy is this moment—don't miss it!" Meditation gets us in touch with that moment by teaching us how to live in the present.

Although meditation has been described as a reflective mode of thought, a more accurate definition would be a mode of "no thought," since the goal of meditation is to journey to a quiet place beyond the thought-filled mind. When we reach this thought-free place, we find peace and happiness. Our daily worries and chattering minds recede into the background and the pure energy of our own being comes into the foreground, letting us experience a complete delight in living.

Meditation is a change of focus from the outer world to the inner world. It has been used for centuries in many philosophical and religious traditions as a way to pray, commune with nature, contemplate God, and as a path to inner peace.

The more we incorporate meditation into our lives, the more we realize how vital it is to a happier, healthier, more conscious existence. It is the key to our inner joy.

Who Meditates?

Meditation has long been a powerful tool for personal growth in the East, and now, in less than twenty years, it has found itself more and more in the mainstream of Western life. It's prescribed and practiced by licensed medical doctors to reduce stress and help in the prevention and healing of various stress-related diseases, from heart trouble and cancer to melancholia, back problems, and ulcers.

Major corporations have integrated stress reduction programs into their agendas and have found that by introducing meditation-based techniques, production improves and people function more efficiently.

Athletes are meditating to improve their game, and due to phenomenal findings in the world of physics, some of our foremost scientists are now experimenting with meditation. People in the arts find that meditation puts them more in touch with their creativity, and people who teach find that they have more patience and a better outlook in dealing with their students. Regardless of the many reasons people meditate, the results are the same—an experience of inner peace, joy, and tranquility.

One of the great things about meditation is you don't have to take anyone's word about the beneficial effects. You can try it yourself. This is a practice in which the practitioner is his own laboratory.

When you meditate, you're not dependent on anything but your own self. When you still the mind by meditating, it becomes more powerful and focused. The energy expended in letting the mind wander here and there is conserved. When your mind isn't cluttered with random thoughts and worries, you become much clearer and better able to cope, even when major problems confront you. Meditation enables you to develop and maintain an inner balance and sense of peace.

Your Journey

The journey toward inner peace begins with an exploration of your current state, your goals and desires, hopes and fears, attractions and distractions. From here you'll be traveling to the more subtle realms of the inner world by learning to redirect and focus your attention. Since meditation is about making the mind very still, you can experience the peace that underlies it by becoming acquainted with your mind. New ways of listening to sound as well as to your own mind and body are also explored for the purpose of guiding you more deeply into the silence of meditation.

By using this book as a road map, you will be guided through each stage of your inner venture. Each chapter explores different levels of your experience and in doing so, guides you more deeply into meditation and gives you a greater awareness of your own mind. As you journey inward, you'll find that there are many surprises; many experiences where joy is waiting to unfold.

Throughout the book you'll find a variety of short focused meditations called "inner," "outer," or "special" focus, which let you experience all the different routes to the peace and joy hidden within you. The outer focuses accomplish this by showing you what keeps you from this space. Inner focuses are the vehicles to get you there. Special focuses provide effective ways to deal with stress, muscle tension, and other problems; essentially, they're quick pick-me-ups.

Each chapter concludes with a mini-meditation that is designed to stretch your meditation muscles and to help you assimilate the experiences you've had throughout the chapter.

In all of these exercises, you'll be focusing your attention in new ways that will allow you to experience meditation more easily. As you practice each exercise, you'll find that meditation is very familiar to you. That's because it's similar to daydreaming and just a step away from a good night's sleep.

You may find that some of the exercises are similar to each other. As in any journey, the more often we take the same route, the easier the trip becomes. We begin to notice the different signposts along the way that let us know we're going in the right direction. Each practice session will make the space of meditation more and more familiar, and your moods lighter and lighter.

Unlike other activities that exhaust your energy, meditation restores and expands it. The overall benefit of meditation is that this energy stays with you. The more you use it, the more it grows.

To help you log your progress throughout the book, keep a notebook handy—it's a fun way to explore your experiences in meditation. You'll also find it useful for several of the inner and outer focus exercises. Some of these techniques may suit your temperament better than others and as you try each one, you may also want to make a note of which work best for you.

Once you've completed all of the focus techniques and mini-meditations, you'll be more conscious of your outer world, more familiar with your inner world, and ready to explore the deeper levels of meditation. To guide you in this exploration, we've prepared a four-week daily practice program which you'll find at the end of the book.

Daily Meditation

After you've read chapters 1 through 6, you'll be ready for daily meditation. The four-week program builds on the meditation experiences you've had throughout the book and initiates the habit of daily practice. It incorporates all of the elements of the inner and outer focuses and mini-meditations and takes you through a planned progression of visualization and breathing exercises that enable you to sit in meditation for longer periods of time. Daily practice is designed to take you to even deeper levels of meditation.

You'll begin with fifteen-minute meditations and increase by five minute increments to thirty minutes by the fourth week. As you continue to meditate, you'll find that the benefits of daily practice are immediately evidenced by a calmer mind and a more relaxed body.

Joy Is this Moment

Any of the meditations we've included in this book can be used for daily meditation. Many of the focusing techniques can be incorporated into your daily life—at work or at home—to help you relax wherever you are! If you use these exercises to help you stay aligned with your own inner joy, without a doubt your life will become more joyful. The more joy you experience within yourself, the more you can share with others.

Set aside some quality time to work with this book and choose a place where you won't be disturbed. Make this time a gift to yourself.

May meditation become your key to happiness.

• 1 •

The Search for Happiness

Happiness is considered to be such a fundamental right that the Declaration of Independence even guarantees us the freedom to pursue it. And we do, chasing that elusive thing called happiness wherever we think we can find it.

Everyone *wants* to be happy, but few people ever feel they're totally happy. There's always something missing. So we find ourselves either looking for that missing ingredient or lamenting its lack.

For some people happiness can be the sight of a rose, the first signs of spring, or a beautiful sunset, while for others it's nothing less than a new car or money in the bank. It can mean having everything we want or need or having everything we *think* we want or need.

Over the years, people who meditate have discovered that there is a source of inner happiness that is more lasting than what we pursue in the outside world. As soon as we discover this vast spiritual wealth, life begins to fall into place and our inner happiness begins to spill over into our outer activities. This is the result of meditation.

Meditation isn't a substitute for having money in the bank or the sight of a rose, but it does enhance those experiences when we have them, and it keeps us aware of the lasting happiness within when we don't.

What Makes You Happy?

When we asked people to tell us what makes them happy, we got a wide variety of answers.

> Money, money. Money makes me happy.
>
> SY, 43, graphic artist

> Besides sex? Making a living with my singing.
>
> JG, 25, receptionist/singer

> M&M's, playing with my niece, being with my boyfriend.
>
> HG, 27, dental receptionist

> Dancing, dancing, dancing.
>
> CS, 42, social worker

> Music makes me happy. Attention makes me real happy, too. And laughing—it's very therapeutic.
>
> ST, 42, fund-raiser

> Going into a shoe store and finding exactly what I was looking for in the right size, marked down three times.
>
> DK, 36, jeweler

> Animals. Being out in nature, being out in the wild, makes me ecstatic. And knitting. Knitting makes me happy, too.
>
> BG, 44, manager

> Being with someone I can share thoughts with and enjoy things with.
>
> CP, 31, psychotherapist

> Planning for the future.
>
> CO, 44, banker

There can be as many answers to the question "What makes you happy?" as there are people. Now you're going to experience whatever it is that makes *you* happy. However, instead of experiencing it as a physical reality, you'll be experiencing it mentally by using a focusing technique.

The first exercise is two-fold, an outer focus followed by an inner focus. The outer focus will give you an insight into the workings of your own mind, and the inner focus will use this experience to take you to a new level of awareness. These creative focuses, or visualization techniques, are designed to redirect your thoughts and your senses to the place of meditation. The inner focuses throughout this book are all light-level meditations that take place at the alpha level of consciousness, where the brain waves measure eight to twelve waves per second. This is the state of deep relaxation. It's the level you've visited in daydreams and, in fact, every time you blink your eyes you experience the alpha state. When you function at this level with a particular focus or purpose, you come out feeling refreshed and happy.

To get the maximum benefit from the inner and outer focuses or any of the meditational exercises in this book, read them through a few times to set them in your mind. Take your time with these exercises. After each inner, outer, or special focus, relax and think about what you've experienced. One way to reinforce your experiences at the alpha level is by writing down your impressions, observations, or changes in your mood after each exercise, so keep a notebook handy.

Outer Focus: What Makes Me Happy
Spend a few minutes thinking about your own search for happiness. What are the things that bring joy into your life? It could be a sunset, a person, a painting, an activity. You may find that thinking about what makes you happy brings a smile to your lips and a feeling of lightness.

Write down all the things you thought of. Look at your

list. Does anything on the list surprise you? Is there anything you've left out?

Next, you'll be using your imagination to visualize one of the things you just thought about. Review your list and select one item to focus on. Pick the one that makes you happiest of all.

Sitting in a quiet place where you won't be disturbed will always be your first step toward meditation. Just spending a few moments with your eyes closed creates a feeling of peace.

Inner Focus: The Experience of Happiness

Sitting comfortably, with your spine straight, close your eyes and breathe deeply and evenly. Picture whatever it is that makes you the happiest. Focus all of your attention on it. If it's being with a particular person, envision yourself sharing a wonderful moment with her. Create it fully in your mind and feel it in your heart. How does it feel? If it's a sunset or a painting or a flower, envision that and focus on how it makes you feel inside. If it's an activity, see yourself involved in it and try to recapture the feeling it awakens in you. Picture it as fully as possible. Stay focused on this mental image and the feeling it creates. Give yourself time to totally experience what you're feeling and discover the place inside where that feeling springs from.

Do you feel peaceful? Lighter? Happier? Take a few minutes to write down in your notebook anything you may have observed or felt during this experience.

By focusing on what makes you happy, you entered a light level of meditation where you could experience that happiness inside yourself. The power of meditation is its ability to release tremendous joy and happiness from within—yet this is usually the last place one looks.

In India they tell a story about the musk deer, which has a beautiful fragrance emanating from its navel. The deer falls in love with this fragrance and, not knowing that the source is its own navel, it runs through the forest in search of the intoxicating scent until it collapses in exhaustion.

As we look hither and yon for the things that we feel will make us happy, we're very much like that musk deer. Meditation can help us find our source of happiness and experience joy without being dependent on the external world. This doesn't mean that we're hiding from the world, rather, we're integrating our inner joy with our outer experience.

So what keeps us from looking within?

The Wrong Direction

Our search for happiness outside of ourselves begins very early. It is essential to our development to have our senses stimulated; without that stimulation, we don't learn or grow. So from a very early age we naturally become outer focused, relating to the world only through our senses. As infants, our very survival depends on outside forces. Our senses are continually stimulated with new information—we're fed, touched, spoken to; we explore our toes, people's faces, the sound of our own voices.

As we get older, it seems that our happiness is dependent on the love of our parents, our popularity among our peers, our academic achievements, athletic prowess, and the number and quality of our clothes and possessions. As adults our senses continue to want gratification and stimulation, but our desires have become more complex—security, fame, money, marriage, children, friends, lovers, a job, prestige. We still tend to equate our happiness with the people, objects, relationships, and activities we think can help us attain it.

Society supports this outer search by constantly inundating us with new images to desire. We are bombarded with new ways to experience a rush, to feel joy; to find romance; to discover paradise in an exotic vacation, expensive wardrobe, more jewelry, or a better paying job.

While reading the newspapers, or a magazine, or while watching TV this week, note the number of ads that offer you happiness. Notice your reactions to them. Do they make you want to buy whatever is being offered? Do they make you feel hungry? Incomplete? The new car that takes you anywhere faster, the perfume that guarantees a lasting relationship, the jewelry that makes you feel like royalty—we're constantly flooded with commercials on radio and TV that promise us nothing less than eternal happiness. But often when we buy these things, our happiness doesn't last. And if we can't go out and buy the things we see, we may even feel deprived.

When we know that our happiness comes from inside, we can always dive in and come out feeling refreshed. For example, a trip to Bermuda during a cold gray winter may be particularly appealing, but it may not be feasible to hop a plane and follow that dream. What you *can* do instead is turn within and use the beauty of a Bermuda beach as an inner focus. You can emerge from that rather brief journey wonderfully relaxed and contented, with a nice warm glow. All you'll be missing is the tan. If we can take the trip, fine, but if not, we don't have to bemoan our fate.

If we limit our focus to the outside world, the world of the senses, we become dependent upon it for our happiness. When we redirect our senses by turning within, we discover the happiness of our own inner world and find we're not dependent on anything. Visualization is a common way of doing this.

You're already familiar with this technique from the first exercise in this chapter. The next inner focus will give you a chance to practice visualization again as well as give you a deeper understanding of your desires. This time, you're going to focus on a wish you would like to come true. Remember, in the mind, anything is possible, so let your imagination soar.

This is a three-part exercise, so make sure you have at least thirty minutes before beginning. First, you'll use an outer focus technique, then a two-part inner focus. You'll need your notebook and pen for this one.

Outer Focus: My Wish List

Sitting comfortably, close your eyes and take a few minutes to think of all the things you desire—cars, diamonds, money, jobs, relationships. What wish would you like to come true?

When you're ready, open your eyes and write down all of the things that you want most in this world that you don't have. Number them in order of importance, with number one being the thing you want most.

Once your list is complete, go over each thing and give it serious thought. Really consider everything on your list. Ask yourself:

Do I really need it?
How will this improve my life?
How long will this keep me happy?
Would I be happier if I didn't accumulate more
     bills by getting this?
If Joe Smith didn't have one, would I want one?
If I didn't see one everywhere I looked, would I
     want one?
What do I really want and what do I think the
     world is telling me I should want?

Spend a few minutes writing down any thoughts you have about each item on the list and any general thoughts you may have as you look at your wish list. Give yourself up to ten minutes for this part.

Once you've carefully considered what you want most in the outside world, you're going to explore what it feels like to actually have it, by going within to get it.

What wish would you most like to come true?

Inner Focus: The Wish-Fulfilling Tree

Sitting comfortably with your spine straight, close your eyes and take a few long, deep breaths to clear your mind. Keeping your eyes closed, picture a blank movie or TV screen. Select whatever is number one on your list and see it on the screen. Visualize having this desire fulfilled. Take the time to picture it fully. If the desire is for a diamond, picture the diamond in your hand. Look at it closely, see the many facets catching the light. If it's a car, see it sitting before you, or imagine yourself sitting in it. What does it feel like? What color is it? If it's a dress, a suit, a coat, a boat, or a person, picture it in the same detail. See whatever it is you want as clearly as possible. See it as having arrived on your doorstep just as you had always imagined it.

Gaze inwardly at your heart's desire for as long as possible. How do you feel inside? You have everything. Nothing is lacking in your life. Stay with that feeling of fullness for a few minutes before going on.

Take a moment now to write down any thoughts, observations, or revelations about your desires and notice how you're feeling now as compared to how you felt before doing the exercise.

In the second part of this inner focus, you'll be leaving your desires behind. Close your eyes again and clear your mind by taking a few long, even breaths. This time, picture a beautiful flower, a sunset, a waterfall, a full moon, anything in nature that delights you. Picture whatever scene you choose completely. If it's a flower, see the petals, the color, the texture. If it's a sunset, see the beautiful colors, and how the colors tint the land or water. See the waterfall with a fine mist all around it, and rainbows dancing in the mist.

Whichever scene from nature you choose, see it in as much detail as possible. It doesn't have to be one of the above scenes. Choose a scene that's special to you and focus on it inwardly.

How do you feel? Do you feel peaceful? Joyous? Keep your eyes closed and stay with that feeling for as long as possible.

You Can't Beat Mother Nature

Both of these exercises let you experience the joy unleashed by meditating. It is likely, though, that the nature exercise gave you a feeling which was more peaceful and more expansive than the exercise in which you focused on fulfilling your desires. This may be because the wish you focused on carried a hidden agenda—like wanting something because it would bring prestige. Nature, on the other hand, extends its beauty with no strings attached. It's freely given and freely enjoyed.

We're uplifted by natural beauty, because our own inner nature responds. This is why country getaways are so refreshing. When viewing a mountain etched against the setting sun, or the moon casting its light across the water, we get a welling up of happiness. In these moments we don't think of wanting anything.

In truth, every moment of our lives holds the potential for happiness; it's there for the taking, all we have to do is let it in. When we take a moment to sit peacefully and make our minds very still, we see that there's really nothing lacking. Then the things we buy and do, and the relationships we have are like bonuses. We don't *need* them for completion because we're already complete.

Letting Go

We can still work toward our dreams and explore our desires, but we don't have to let our desires keep us from experiencing our inner joy. When we can enjoy the world as it is, instead of how we would like it to be, our lives become happier.

If you have any unfulfilled wishes or desires that are causing you to feel a lack, this next meditation will help free you up. We're not talking about things you need, we're talking about the extra things you want but could easily live without.

You'll be using your imagination once again as a point of focus that allows you to experience a deeper part of yourself.

Take at least five minutes for this exercise, but spend as much time on it as you need.

Go back to your wish list and this time determine if there's anything on the list that you really don't need. Remember, if you think you need something, you won't be satisfied until you get it. If you realize you don't need it, then there's no lack, no dissatisfaction, and you'll find you're actually happy without it. In this next meditation, you'll be letting go of any desire that you *think* stands between you and your happiness.

Inner Focus: Letting Go of What You Don't Need

Once you've determined which desires are holding you back or keeping you from being happy, close your eyes and sitting comfortably, see each wish or desire as a brightly colored helium-filled balloon. What color does a particular desire evoke? If it's red, turn that desire into a big red balloon and in big letters name the desire. See yourself letting go of the string connecting you to the desire. Watch as the balloon and string drift off into the sky becoming smaller and smaller. At the same time, feel yourself becoming lighter and lighter.

Perhaps you have a desire for a mountain of money, or you might feel continually anxious about not having enough money. You can see that desire as a green balloon. Picture yourself holding a big green helium-filled balloon. Label it with a dollar sign and then let go of the string.

You may want to make your desires all one color. Or as you picture the balloon, a color may arise spontaneously. Watch as the balloon floats away and disappears into the sky. As each balloon disappears, feel yourself getting lighter and lighter.

Anytime desires make you restless, or cause you to feel that you're lacking something, just come back to this exercise. Letting go of what you don't have can create the space for something better to come into your life.

The Key to Happiness

To synthesize what you've learned in this chapter and deepen your level of meditation, in the next exercise you'll be going back to the first inner focus and taking it one step further.

Once again, think about whatever it is that makes you happiest.

Mini-Meditation: Resting in the Joy

Sitting comfortably, with your spine erect, close your eyes and take a few deep breaths. Picturing a blank TV or movie screen will help to clear your mind.

Focus your attention on the person or object or activity that makes you happiest. Again, create it fully in your mind as you did in the earlier focus. As you begin to experience the feeling of happiness inside, turn your focus to the feeling. Allow this feeling of happiness to expand until it fills you completely with a sense of well-being. Then rest in this sense of well-being for as long as it lasts.

As you redirect your attention away from the image to the feeling of happiness itself, the feeling expands and you experience the source of happiness within.

Meditation returns us to our essentially joyous nature by connecting us to this source. When we connect to this space inside, we can enjoy our possessions and external pleasures, but we're freed from believing that we need these things to be happy.

By doing the focuses in this section, you've not only experienced light-level meditations, you've had a chance to examine your own hopes, dreams, and goals and to discover a glimpse of the true happiness inside you.

As you continue to do the inner and outer focuses in the following chapters, you will become more and more familiar with this amazing inner resource.

· 2 ·

Learning to Focus

In meditation we focus the mind so that no thoughts get in the way of our inner happiness. There are many techniques available to assist you in achieving this state and just as many mental obstacles to overcome in obtaining it. Focusing on a mental image, as you did in chapter 1, or on the breath or a point in space are the more well-known methods for silencing the mind. This kind of intense inner focus gets easier with practice. In our external lives, we do it all the time.

We've all had the experience of intense focus when instead of running wild, all our senses are engaged by only one thing—studying for an exam, watching TV, or even playing a game. At these times, we may have found that nothing distracts us from what we're doing, we don't even hear what's going on around us. How many times have you been so absorbed in what you were doing that you didn't even hear your name being called?

Dr. Seymour Epstein, a psychologist at the University of Massachusetts claims, "being totally absorbed is in itself pleasurable. Complete concentration that blanks out everything else temporarily relieves you from all conflicts. Even if it's scary, it's a way to drive out disturbing thoughts."

The popularity of horror films and thrill rides supports

this theory. Watching a scary movie or going on a roller coaster ride drives out all other thoughts. For a moment, we become so utterly focused that the mind is still.

Dr. Epstein goes on to say, "It makes you feel very alive to be so scared. When you react to something that demands your full attention so forcefully, all your senses engage. It's a very different feeling from being in your usual semi-awake state." That semiawake state comes from reacting to what is going on in our minds rather than focusing on whatever is happening in the moment.

The Peak Experience

Daredevils and stuntmen are familiar with the exhilaration intense focus can release. The kind of concentration required to attempt death-defying feats leaves absolutely no room for the mind to chatter on and on. The mind must be still, the focus must be constant, or disaster results.

When we're so intensely focused we may experience a state of altered consciousness or what psychologist Abraham Maslow refers to as a peak experience. Maslow states, "In the peak experience, such emotions as wonder, awe, reverence, humility, surrender, and even worship before the greatness of the experience are often reported." Just as a magnifying glass focused in the sun's rays releases the burning power of the sun and can cause a rope to burst into flames, our senses, when totally engaged, release the power of our own inner bliss.

Athletes often experience an altered state as a result of their intense focus on performance. For runners this is sometimes called a "runner's high." This total engagement of the senses releases feelings of well-being and one's abilities seem to expand.

Brazilian soccer champion Pele spoke of the experience as a "strange calmness. A type of euphoria." During one of these periods he also felt that he could run all day and could not be hurt.

A friend who heads a very successful real estate operation in New York leaves the concrete jungle behind to ride the surf whenever time allows. According to him, "There's no way you can have any other thoughts," when riding that wave, "you don't think of anything. It's like being in a capsule, almost noiseless . . . a feeling of euphoria."

People who meditate have reported similar experiences. However, in meditation, the focus is turned inward instead of outward. Whether you realize it or not, you've probably experienced an altered state of consciousness at some point in your life. Have you ever fallen madly in love?

Drunk on Love

When we're "madly" in love, suddenly the whole world looks beautiful. Our senses become totally absorbed in our beloved and we experience a divine inner intoxication and bliss. We "walk on clouds," we "walk on air," we're "several stories high," we're "younger than springtime." We've met someone who, for a moment, stops our mind's desires. The mind becomes focused and love pours out. And while it appears as if the other person has caused this feeling to happen to us, in fact, it is our own love being released because of the total engagement of the mind and senses.

You can experience this same dance of the heart by turning your focus inward. The love that you feel really does come from inside. The more you practice focusing on that inner love, the more it will pervade your daily life.

To experience the power of this love within, the next meditation will have love as its focus. But first, you're going to learn a breathing technique that will deepen the experience for you.

The breath is a great vehicle for getting you into meditation. Long, deep breaths have a calming effect on the body and help slow the torrent of thoughts in the mind. Use this technique to center yourself before each inner and outer focus exercise.

Outer Focus: Expanding the Breath

Sitting comfortably, spine erect, close your eyes. Begin taking deep and even breaths. As you inhale, your abdomen should protrude outward slightly and your rib cage should expand a bit. To make sure you are breathing correctly, place a hand just below the rib cage and feel your abdomen press slightly against it as you inhale. Exhale slowly and evenly feeling the abdomen and rib cage contracting. Repeat this two or three times, until you get the hang of it.

Each breath should be full—pushing the abdomen out slightly and expanding the rib cage. This shouldn't be a strain, just a nice, slow even breath in and out.

Inner Focus: Feeling the Love Inside

Using the breathing technique you just learned, take a few deep breaths to center yourself and then focus your awareness on whatever it is that makes you feel love. Recall your deepest experience of love. Was it embracing someone? Feeling your heart melt at a baby's smile? Holding a warm, soft, velvety little puppy? Focus on anything in your life that filled your heart with love. Focus on this experience until you feel that love in all its fullness, then focus on the feeling of that love. Let its warm glow begin to radiate within your heart. Feel it expanding as you breathe. Feel love filling you up within. Let its warmth permeate your body.

As you breathe, feel love move through your arms out to your fingertips. Take it all the way through your torso down to your thighs, your legs, and your toes. Let love reach every corner of your being. Feel yourself as love. Stay with that feeling for as long as possible.

❧

Do you feel a warm glow? Are you smiling from the inside out? Write down all of the thoughts and feelings that arose as a result of this meditation. Just by focusing that love, its presence is evoked. The more you practice this meditation, the more love will radiate from you. The intensity of your focus will determine the intensity of your experience. In doing these meditations, you will become familiar with the place of perfect love inside. As you continue to practice, it will be easier to access. By practicing in our minds, we not only improve our mental states, but we can also improve our physical performance.

Practice Makes Perfect

Athletes have found that mental practice very often enhances physical practice. For this reason, meditation has become an integral part of physical training for many athletes.

Experiments in basketball in the Soviet Union reveal that athletes who spend time on mental training perform better than athletes whose practice and exercise is primarily physical. In one experiment, one team practiced shooting for baskets on the court every day, one team didn't practice at all, and the third team practiced by visualizing themselves getting the basket through the hoop. The results showed 24 percent improvement in the team that practiced on the court, no improvement for the one that didn't practice at all, and 23 percent improvement for the team that practiced mentally.

As a result of this type of research, books offering techniques for mental practice have been written to help athletes improve their sports skills. W. Timothy Gallwey's *The Inner Game of Tennis* advances techniques that allow the game of tennis to take place within the mind of the player as a means of preparation for the outer game, and *Inner Skiing* by W. Timothy Gallwey and Bob Kriegel promises to "unlock your ability to 'ski out of your mind.' "

Teenage Olympic archery champion Denise Parker uses the inward focus provided by meditation as part of her training. This meditative training consists of retiring to her "happiness" room. In this room, which her own mind has created and furnished with all her favorite things, Denise visualizes watching herself on a VCR releasing perfect shots over and over again. Both she and her trainer are convinced that this technique enhances her performance.

Regardless of how we earn our livings or spend our time, we can all have "happiness" rooms in which to work on whatever it is we wish to accomplish.

The following meditation is one in which focusing becomes a tool to help you improve your life. By focusing on the practice of any skill in your mind, be it dancing, sports, or typing you create an energy that improves the skill. The part of the brain from which the action is directed reacts as though the body is actually going through the training.

Special Focus: Your Practice Room

Sitting comfortably with your spine erect, close your eyes, and take a few deep, even breaths using the breathing technique you learned earlier. Focusing your awareness within, create the perfect dream room for yourself—one that contains everything you need to bring you peace and happiness. See it in all its detail. Color, shape, wall texture, furnishings, windows. It's your room, so create it exactly as you wish. Spend ten minutes creating your room.

This will be a room that you can come to for solving problems, for a focus for meditation, for practicing whatever it is that you would like to gain skill in, or for healing yourself if you're working on a physical problem. Merely being in this room will reduce the stress that so often causes illness or interferes with our performing at optimal levels.

This is your room to come to whenever you want. You may want to keep a log of any revelations you have while in this space. Try spending time in your room over the next few weeks and write down your experiences after each session. Notice if it makes any inroads in your daily life.

The Thought-Free State

When we can control thoughts through focusing we can accomplish a lot. However, as powerful as our thoughts may be, they can only take us so far in meditation. Just as focusing on a single thought can help us improve a skill, emptying the mind of all thoughts improves our whole life by taking us even deeper within.

The goal of meditation is to reach the thought-free place within. When we're able to reach this place of inner silence, our joy expands because there's nothing to stop it—no concepts, no worries, no fears. When your thoughts don't get in the way, your inner joy wells up inside giving you an incredible feeling of wholeness and happiness. This tremendous feeling affects you on all levels of your being.

When we focus our energies on attaining this thought-free state in meditation, even our problems are experienced in a different way.

Hidden Treasure

A colleague had a dramatic experience of this kind recently. She was on deadline for an article and had the weekend to finish it. Her mate, also a writer, had the maddening habit of not turning off the typewriter switch when he finished writing. She constantly admonished him that the motor would burn out if he continued to be careless about this.

On this glorious weekend, while he was out enjoying the weather, she sat down to finish the article. She turned the machine on. The typewriter was dead. No motor. Nothing.

She checked the wall outlet, it was plugged in. And by now so was she! There were no repair shops to go to, no rental places—it was a weekend! Not only was she afraid of missing her deadline, she also found herself being consumed by anger at her mate. Suddenly she realized she was the one who was suffering from her anger. It wasn't hurting him one bit. He was out enjoying the day with his friends.

At this point, just to make herself feel better, she decided to meditate. In the middle of her anxiety and anger, she sat down and closed her eyes, emptying her mind of all thoughts. Within ten minutes, a real-as-life picture spontaneously appeared in her mind. It was the back of the typewriter, with a plug sitting alongside it.

Sure enough, when she looked, the typewriter cord was plugged into the wall, but it wasn't plugged into the typewriter at the other end. It hadn't occurred to her to check the plug into the typewriter; she assumed it was built in.

If we allow our minds to lead us on fictional journeys we are bound to suffer. If we turn our focus within, we come out refreshed and joyful. Being a meditator, our colleague recognized that she didn't have to continue the frenzied reaction her mind was setting up; she had the option of cooling out by turning within. She never expected anything more than feeling refreshed, so having a solution appear was a terrific bonus.

When we meditate, the energy expended in letting anxiety and worry overcome us is replaced by calmly handling whatever obstacles present themselves.

An executive with a high pressure job says she can't function without her morning meditation. Often she'll remember something that has to get done that day that she'd totally forgotten. "Sometimes it's a meeting, or a critical phone call that I have to make but forgot to write down. It was just the kind of thing that I'd forget in the course of a hectic day. But now that I meditate, suddenly the thought will just pop up—call your mother, it's her birthday!"

A young mother of two says that her husband, although he doesn't meditate himself, thinks that it's great that she does. "He noticed the change in me," she says. "I'm much calmer and I feel a lot happier. I don't let all the little things that used to upset me get to me anymore. They just don't bother me, but even if they do, I make the time to sit and meditate and I always feel better afterward."

Finding Center

The thought-free place we find in meditation is the center of our being. This center is the source of all energy. In Japan, it's called *ki*. The alignment of certain body movements with the *ki* is the basis of karate. Such power is unleashed by someone who has mastered this martial art that a karate black belt must register her hands with the police as lethal weapons. In China, this energy is called *chi* and is the center from which Chinese martial arts derive their power. In India, this energy is called *shakti* and is worshipped in its many different forms as the power that creates the universe. In every culture this energy has been identified and acknowledged as being all powerful, all knowing, and present in all things.

One of the ways to reach this core of energy within is through focusing on the breath. In the next exercise, you'll use a breathing technique to still the mind, so that you can begin to experience this inner power. You'll be expanding on the technique you learned at the beginning of the chapter to help you focus. Focusing your attention on the breath is a common centering technique and will help you reach that thought-free state where you can experience that powerful energy inside.

Give yourself ten minutes with this exercise.

Mini-Meditation: Using the Breath to Find Center
Sitting comfortably with your spine erect, close your eyes and begin breathing deeply and evenly. Focus your atten-

tion on your breathing. At first, to help you focus, as you inhale repeat silently to yourself "inhale" and as you exhale, repeat silently to yourself "exhale."

Continue to breathe deeply and evenly, your awareness focused on the breath as it comes in and goes out. As you focus in this way, you'll find that in between the inhale and the exhale is a momentary pause. Focus your attention on this split second between breaths where you are neither inhaling nor exhaling, but you are *not* holding your breath. The space between breaths is the thought-free state. Continue to breathe but concentrate your attention on that moment of pause, that split second when you are neither inhaling nor exhaling.

Each time you reach that moment of pause, focus on it for as long as you can. Watch this pause as it grows longer. Any time you become aware of thoughts distracting you, gently return your attention to the breath.

How do you feel? Relaxed? Calmer? Refreshed? Energized? Write down any experiences you may have had in this meditation. Is there a difference between how you feel now and your usual state of consciousness?

As you've been discovering, there are many different focusing techniques to draw you into meditation. It doesn't matter which one you use, the end result is the same—we regain our connection to ourselves and experience peak moments without doing anything out of the ordinary.

In meditation we find the true center of our being. Just as a wheel can't function without a hub, we also can't function without our own hub, or center. When we find the true center of our being through the practice of meditation, we breathe a sigh of relief. From this perspective, we're able to enjoy life from a front row seat and flow more easily with the constant changes that life presents.

· 3 ·

The World of the Mind

It is only when we try to silence the mind through meditation that we become aware of the steady hum of thoughts our minds are immersed in all the time. You may have become aware of this as you practiced the meditations in the first two chapters. If you did notice thoughts taking your attention away from your meditation, you're well on your way to being able to detach your mind from those distracting thoughts. It's only when you become aware of this constant intrusion on your inner state that you can detach from it.

This chapter will take you through a variety of techniques that will open up new doors of awareness for you. By using these meditative techniques, you can begin to recognize the difference between your thoughts and the silent background that is your own inner self. In meditation, you can connect with this inner self and witness your thoughts as they arise and dissolve.

Normally we identify so closely with what we're thinking, we don't even realize we're thinking. Our thought forms are so powerful, we become caught up in them and we are pulled out of that inner peace and quiet. It's like being buffeted about by hurricane winds instead of being in the eye of the storm where it's tranquil. One of the goals of

29

meditation is to help one remain calm no matter what life brings.

Hanging On

When the mind is brought under control and used constructively, it can be a very powerful instrument. If we bring it into sharp focus, rather than let it dart around randomly, we can accomplish a great deal with a minimum of effort.

One friend shared that he used to have a recurring nightmare about hanging from a branch that was rooted in loose earth. As he hung on for dear life, suspended over a sheer drop, the root continued to pull away from the loosened earth bringing him dangerously close to death. Each time he had this dream he would wake up in a sweat.

The last time he had the dream, as the root was tearing away from the earth, instead of holding on with his eyes squeezed shut in fear, something made him look down into the pit he was suspended over. He could hardly believe what he saw when he looked down: The bottom of the pit was no more than six inches beneath him. All that time, in all those dreams, he was hanging on in mortal fear, when at any time, if he had only opened his eyes, he would have seen that he could have just let go and walked away.

This is something we all do. We hang on. We hang on to our thoughts, we hang on to all the things we've created in our minds—all of the fantasies, the worries, the fears—and feel helpless. We never look at why we think the way we do, we just keep hanging in there with our eyes closed. These mental habits hold us back from taking the steps that will free us to lead happier lives.

Mind Games

The way we think is so ingrained in us that it is not always easy to change. One of the most recent techniques for changing our thought patterns is listening to self-improvement audiotapes. There are tapes to help you stop smoking or eating, tapes to help you sleep, or feel your own power, tapes for creating a more prosperous or creative you. These tapes help us reprogram our behavior by giving us affirmations that tell us we have the power to make changes in our lives. In the same way, our daily thoughts also program us. We can use our minds to enhance our experiences or we may find that our thought patterns serve only to limit us and remind us of our shortcomings.

We can all develop good mental habits by being aware of the types of thoughts that fill our minds. Meditation is a good mental habit because it allows us to witness our thoughts instead of becoming entangled in them. It allows us to merge with our inner energy instead of draining it. As we begin to watch our thoughts rather than getting caught up in the mind's play, we begin to gain mastery over our minds.

So often we allow our minds to interfere with our happiness. We forget about what's making us happy now and start anticipating the next thing that we hope to enjoy. We're so in the habit of living in our minds that we lose the precious moments of the present.

Each and every moment has the potential for joy. Meditation teaches us how to discover this joy in every moment by detaching from the thoughts that stir up needless fear and worry.

What's on Your Mind?

Many different techniques have been developed to help people detach from their thoughts—breathing exercises, focusing, and the repetition of certain sounds, among others. However, an essential first step is becoming more aware of the kind of thoughts that fill your mind. What is it you think about?

The next exercise will help you gain a new awareness of your mind by taking a closer look at it. You may find that as you look at your thoughts head on, they disappear. Observing your thoughts makes it easier to gain power over them.

Spend at least ten minutes on the next exercise. You'll need your notebook for this one.

Outer Focus: Becoming the Witness

Sitting comfortably, close your eyes. Try *not* to think of anything. Focus on your breathing. Watch the breath as it comes in and goes out. As you continue to focus on your breathing, you'll find that one by one thoughts will present themselves. Each time this happens, stop and write down the thought. Then close your eyes again and return to focusing on the breath until the next thought arises. Continue doing this for about ten minutes. It doesn't matter how important or trivial or embarrassing they may seem to you, just write them down and return to the exercise.

Are you surprised at how many thoughts arose in ten minutes of sitting still? What kind of thoughts were they? Old? New? Problems? Fantasies? Spend a few minutes now reflecting and/or writing about the thoughts that came up for you. Do you recognize any recurring thought patterns or a subject that colors your emotions?

As you can see, one thought after another parades through your awareness—some scary, some funny, some depressing, some loving. The variety is endless. What would have happened if you had allowed yourself to go on a journey with the first thought? For one thing, the list would not have gotten written. For another, you wouldn't be aware of the fact that you were getting lost in your thoughts. This stream of thoughts dissipates our natural storehouse of energy by leading us away from the inner joy which is our center.

Now that you've begun to create some distance from your thoughts, it will become much easier to detach from them and to remain in the present and be aligned with your inner energy. Merely recognizing that "it is only a thought" weakens its power over you.

The Power of Our Thoughts

Consider your thoughts. You can't touch them, feel them, or smell them. Yet they can actually cause you to react physically. We constantly react to forms in our minds that are not real, have no physical substance, and are our own creation. The following exercise will demonstrate the power of your thoughts.

Inner Focus: The Worlds We Create

Sitting quietly, close your eyes and visualize a brick wall two feet away from you. With your eyes closed see nothing but that brick wall. Whether you look up, down, to the right or left, the solid brick wall is there. Notice your feelings as you look at this solid structure looming in front of you. Open your eyes. How did the brick wall make you feel?

Now close your eyes again. This time you're sitting on the beach looking out at the ocean. Look all the way out to the horizon. Wherever you look there's sea and sky, vast and beautiful. How does this make you feel?

Although there's no brick wall and there's no ocean, you still experience a reaction. Do it again. Spend a minute on the brick wall, then spend a minute on the ocean. Which feels better? Did you find that the wall made you feel hemmed in and cramped, while the ocean let you expand, giving you a feeling of buoyancy?

We create our own brick walls or limitless oceans with the thoughts that constantly flow through our minds.

You Are What You Think

A friend recently shared that there are times when she finds herself sitting at home sulking, wallowing in negative thoughts. One day she asked herself, "Would I choose to think these thoughts? What would I prefer to think? How would I prefer to feel?" She noticed that when she got locked into negative thoughts, she experienced a dark heavy feeling in the stomach area. When she chose the happy thought instead, a lightness began to arise in the heart region. She realized that she always has the choice of what thoughts she wants to keep in her mind. Our thoughts aren't written in stone. But we all seem to have thought tapes that we play over and over again.

As you continue to become more aware of the types of thoughts that most often present themselves in your mind, you can begin to choose those whose company you like and those you wouldn't have as friends. There are as many positive or happy thoughts available as there are negative or obsessive thoughts; all we have to do is recognize the negative thoughts and switch gears. As soon as you become aware that your thoughts are having a negative effect, ask yourself, "Would I deliberately choose these thoughts?" If the answer is no, you can substitute a positive affirmation every time negative thoughts arise. This affirmation can be anything you want it to be—a word or phrase that will uplift you, inspire you, calm you, or even make you smile—whatever works best for you.

The affirmation can be as simple as "Yes," or "Be happy," or "Relax!" or any of the following phrases:

> I can, I will, I shall!
> I'm alive, alert, aglow with life!
> If I have faith, everything will be possible for me.
> Every day in every way, I'm getting better and
>   better.

I have all the strength I need.
It is my right to feel good about myself.

Affirmations are great because you can repeat them to yourself anytime, while walking, eating, or brushing your teeth. This kind of positive reinforcement not only changes your thinking habits, but it can help eliminate negative patterns altogether. The use of a word or phrase as a tool for inner transformation has been used in many different disciplines. In the East, mantras are used to connect to our inner energy, while in the West, people like Norman Vincent Peale and Jose Silva, among others, have helped transform many lives with the use of positive affirmations.

In addition to using the affirmations regularly, you can let go of many of the thoughts that hold you back by practicing the following technique, which is a little more subtle. This one draws you inward and takes you to a place of peace as you identify your limiting thoughts and let them go.

Inner Focus: Thoughts in the Wind

Sitting comfortably with your eyes closed, take a few deep breaths to center yourself using the expanded breathing technique you learned in chapter 2 (pages 27–28). Are any thoughts keeping you from your own joyous nature? Is there a worry that doesn't have to be there? A fear that keeps you from enjoying your life. A feeling that you could be better, smarter, taller—whatever seems to stand in your way. Visualize each of these thoughts as an autumn leaf. Just as a tree sheds its leaves when they're no longer useful, you can shed these thoughts. See yourself offering the leaf to the breeze as you gently blow it off the open palm of your hand. As you visualize blowing the leaf out of your hand, actually purse your lips and blow out, using a nice long breath. Envision the leaf as it disappears into the blue, blue sky. Feel yourself growing lighter as these leaves vanish into air. The more you do this, the lighter you will feel, and the brighter the world will become.

When the last thought is blown away, sit quietly and take inventory of how you're feeling.

You'll find that the more you challenge unwanted thoughts in this way, the less effect they'll have on you. Your mind will become more peaceful, bringing you closer to your meditative energy.

This exercise can be used anytime, anywhere. Whenever limiting thoughts occur, just take a few minutes to close your eyes and blow them away.

I AM

When we gain control over our thoughts it becomes easier to meditate. We are then able to still the mind and experience our underlying consciousness. This silent background is our true nature. When we form a deeper and deeper connection to this place of peace and renewal, we become filled with bliss. Here, nothing is lacking, we're at total peace. This is our essence. We can refer to this conscious energy as our I AM energy, the energy of pure being, with no limitations attached. Not "I am a man, I am a woman, I am a writer, I am a mechanic, I am good, or I am bad," just pure I AM. All of our labels, our concepts of who and what we are, move us away from this energy. When we discard the labels and still the mind through meditation, we become aligned with it.

The great French philosopher René Descartes, grappling with the question of existence, framed his understanding in the statement, "I think, therefore I am." Perhaps it would have been more accurate to state, I AM, therefore I think. Being, or consciousness, precedes thinking. It is the basis from which thought arises.

Picture a very still clear lake reflecting the sun. Now imagine that lake as consciousness in its pure form, totally peaceful. Imagine the perfect reflection of the sun as love and bliss. When the surface of the lake is still, you get a perfect image of the sun. When the wind blows, the surface of the lake ripples and the sun is distorted by the ripples.

This is what happens with our consciousness. The ripples are our thoughts—contractions of that pure consciousness—which do not let us see a clear reflection of that inner sun. Any thought that diminishes pure consciousness takes us away from our inner joy.

Thoughts are spun from the fabric of our being, or the lake of our consciousness. With this awareness, try the next exercise.

Mini-Meditation: Becoming I AM

Sitting comfortably with your eyes closed, take a few deep breaths to center yourself. As a thought arises, watch it. Watch as it dissolves. As you watch your thoughts arise and dissolve, watch with the awareness that these thoughts are wrinkles in your consciousness. Know that you *are* that consciousness and not your individual thoughts. Your consciousness is the pure energy of being—the pure I AM energy.

Each time a thought arises, repeat I AM silently, affirming that you are not your thoughts. You are I AM. Identifying with the words I AM each time a thought arises will put a distance between you and your thoughts.

Once you begin to separate from your thoughts and identify with your consciousness—your I AM energy—you will begin to feel great. Through meditation, instead of chasing your thoughts—or having them chase you—and wasting mental energy, you'll become energized and begin to experience that dynamic force within you.

° 4 °

The World Is As You See It

Just as our thoughts obscure that I AM energy within, they also color our perceptions of the world outside. Our perceptions are influenced by our upbringing, culture, and past experiences. These experiences create a mental framework for our thoughts that we call concepts. These concepts or ideas become our guideposts in life, helping us interpret what goes on around us. Everything is compared to how we think the world is or should be, and then we react accordingly.

A perfect illustration of how these concepts work can be found in an old Zen puzzle. Take your time trying to solve this one but give yourself a full minute before looking at the answer.

ZEN PUZZLE:

Close your eyes and in your mind picture a duck inside a narrow-necked bottle. Now, without breaking the bottle, get the duck out.

After you've gone over it in your mind for a minute, continue reading. Did you give up and feel frustrated or depressed because you always give up? Did you feel elated because you got the answer or think you did? Puzzlement, frustration, enjoyment, or curiosity may be just a few of the feelings you're experiencing and now you're probably impatient because you still don't have the answer. The answer is: The duck is out. Just like that. You put him inside the bottle in your mind, you can take him out the same way. Just see him on the outside of the bottle. Simple! It is easy to get caught up in our mental creations as though they are real. We struggle to get the duck out of the bottle when in fact there's no duck and no bottle. It's all a play of the mind.

Seeing Is Believing

This play of the mind goes on whether or not we're aware of it. Our ideas about the world are often the result of lifelong thinking habits, and therefore we forget to question or reevaluate them.

For instance, a friend was preparing pot roast for dinner. Before putting it in the oven, she sliced off both ends, and with toothpicks, stuck the ends on top of the pot roast. When her daughter asked her why she did it that way, she replied that she had learned to do it that way by watching her mother. As she thought further about it, she realized that she really didn't know why her mother did it that way, so she called her up to ask.

Her mom's reply? "The pan we had was too small, so I always had to cut the ends off to make the roast fit. We didn't have a lot of money back then, so it was easier to cut the ends off the roast rather than buy a new pan."

It's only when you start to question why you might do something a particular way that there's even a slight possibility of breaking out of that habit. In many cases familiar thought patterns keep us from enjoying our lives because they limit how we experience life.

Broadening Your Horizons

An old adage states that travel is a broadening experience. When we travel, we are suddenly confronted with other ways of doing things; ways we hadn't even considered before. It forces us to examine our own concepts and habits. This enlarges our perspective and gives us a wider view of the world and its possibilities.

Without leaving town, we can experiment with this in our own lives. This next exercise can be done anywhere at anytime. This type of waking meditation can bring a new energy and awareness into your daily life.

Outer Focus: Increasing Awareness

Over the next day or two, try something that isn't a part of your everyday routine. Choose something simple. You might try eating something different for breakfast tomorrow morning, or going a different route to work. You could watch a different TV program or not watch TV at all. Remember, keep it simple.

As you try a new way of doing things, you may notice that you become more conscious of your actions instead of operating automatically. You may also discover that you really pay attention to your surroundings or to the taste of something new, and in doing so, everything becomes more vivid. This heightened awareness makes you feel more alive because it keeps you focused on the moment.

Write down some of the reactions you had to doing things differently. Did you feel more stimulated? Was there more energy in doing even the simplest activity? Did your entire experience of the day change?

As we begin to make changes in our lives, we begin to notice subtle shifts in perception. By doing this exercise, you may have gotten a glimpse of how your way of seeing the world can affect your thinking. Now let's take a look at how these perceptions originate.

The Grammar of Life

Remember those early grammar books that explained the difference between the subject and object in a sentence? Well, in the grammar of life, we're the subject and everything else is the object. Whether it's a person, place, or thing, our mother, father, sister, brother, husband, wife, child, dog, or car, it's still an object. Whatever is outside of us is an object, even though our relationship with it is subjective.

Our minds give each of those objects a particular value. Some are love objects, some are hate objects, some we feel neutral about. Look around you. Look at all the objects surrounding you, human and otherwise. Let your eyes rest on each one and silently name them: chair (or blue chair, or flowered chair), carpet, TV, dog (Rover, Spot, Hercules), husband, wife, friend—name everything you see.

Simply naming objects is about as objective as you can get. Consider now that the objects in our lives are objects we have chosen to surround ourselves with. Those choices come from inside of us, therefore they are subjective. In making a personal choice, a value has already been placed on these objects. You've chosen them for a reason. Color, form, size, utility. Whatever the reason, it came from inside you. Take it a step further. Even if you happen to be reading this on a train, plane, or bus, you've chosen the environment you're in at a particular moment. The environment has become your object. Look around you and name the objects in that environment.

The next exercise will give you a chance to explore the nature of your subjectivity. Spend ten or fifteen minutes on this exercise.

Outer Focus: The Experience of Subject/Object
Now that we've established you as the subject and everything else as an object, pick up your notebook and pen.
Choose ten different objects in your field of vision and write
down any thoughts you have about them. Or merely de-
scribe them. Complete this exercise before you continue
reading.

The fact that you chose those particular objects instead of
ten others is subjective. So your list is subjective. What
made you select those objects? See if you can figure out the
reasons. The choices came from your own mind and even
more importantly from your own experience of those objects.

Take something as impersonal as a penny on the floor.
One person might write, "penny," another, "coin," another "new penny" (if it's new), another, "lost penny,"
"face-up penny," "head-up penny," "shiny penny," "tails-
down penny" or "Oh, there's the penny I lost," "Why is
that penny on the floor?" or "I told George to pick that up
before." The penny is the object, the way we see it is
subjective. If we see something as simple as a penny in so
many different ways, imagine how subjective we become
about everything else.

The Monk's Tale

A clear and wonderful illustration of this is a famous Zen
story about an old and wise Zen master whose patience and
wisdom were known far and wide in Japan. His brother, on
the other hand, was just the opposite. Anger and stupidity
had taken up lodging within him at an early age, leaving
room for little else. No doubt the fact that he was blind in
one eye had something to do with his irritability.

The two monk brothers lived together in a temple visited
by many. Tradition was that any wandering monk could

remain in the temple overnight as a guest by winning a
debate on Buddhism with a temple monk. Up until this one
particular night, the older, wise monk handled these challenges, which is how his reputation had spread throughout
Japan. But on the night of this story, the older monk was
very tired from studying scriptures all day, so when a
wandering monk approached the temple, he sent his brother
to handle the debate, with the directive that the dialogue be
held in silence, because of his brother's meager intellect and
short temper.

Not too long afterward, the elder monk saw the visiting
monk running down the road with his brother hot on his
trail. The senior monk intercepted his brother and asked,
"What happened?"

"As soon as we sat down, he made fun of my blindness
by holding up one finger.

"I tried to be polite and congratulate him on having two
eyes by holding up two fingers.

"Ingrate that he was, he further ridiculed me by holding
up three fingers, letting me know that between the two of
us there were only three eyes.

"So I made a fist and was ready to punch him in the nose,
but he got up, the coward, and ran away. And now I'm
trying to catch him."

Finding it hard to believe that a monk would be so
impolite and insensitive, the older monk pursued the fleeing
monk and asked why he was leaving.

"I was defeated by your brother," the monk answered
humbly. "I opened the debate by holding up one finger to
indicate Buddha, the enlightened one.

"Your brother answered by holding up two fingers, one
for Buddha and one for his teachings.

"I then held up three fingers, one for Buddha, one for his
teachings, and one for his followers.

"At that your brother held up his fist in my face repre-
senting Buddha, his teachings, and his followers all being

one. It was clear that he had won the debate, so I'm running off to look for another temple in which to spend the
night."

The two monks are no different from us in their behavior. Each came from his own reservoir of experience—from
the point of view of what was foremost in his mind.

The Forest Not the Trees

In life, we each select whatever it is we want to focus on
and leave everything else in the background. It's a lot like
not seeing the forest for the trees. We can either see the
individual trees, or we can see the forest. We can see ugli-
ness or we can see beauty. We can see Manhattan as an
island or a city. We can then see it as a majestic city full of
energy and excitement, or as a slum-ridden hotbed of crime
and poverty.

However we might feel, we often refuse to let other
possibilities enter our consciousness because of our predis-
position.

Imagine then, how different our experience can be from
the people in another town or state or country. Try to recall
the things you've seen or read about different places on the
globe, and you'll see there's no one way to be. If there
were, we would all be exactly the same.

In his book *Grist for the Mill*, Ram Dass, whose life has
been devoted to mastering the mind, tells of visiting India.
His first stop is Benares, a sacred city in northeast India
where people go to die. In India it is believed that to die
in Benares is to attain heaven. Many aged and infirm
people arrive from all parts of the subcontinent carrying
the few coins it will take to pay for their funeral tied in
a small bag around their waists. When they die, they are
placed on a funeral pyre and floated out onto the sacred
Ganges.

The sight of these thousands of people on the threshold of death, many begging for their last meal, tore at his heart. He left the city filled with pity for them.

Passing through Benares once again, he suddenly had an entirely different perspective. He realized that the beggars truly believed that death in Benares was a blessing. Furthermore, as he walked the streets once again, he noticed that the same beggars he had pitied were looking at him with pity. From their point of view, he was the unfortunate one and they were the fortunate ones; after all, they were going to die in Benares and he wasn't.

The ancient Indian scriptures say, "The world is as you see it." The way you see it is your truth, your reality. We each come from our own experience and we place that experience on the people and objects in our lives while they're busy doing the same to us. Since each person sees the world through his own eyes, there are as many truths and realities as there are people on the planet.

The more we can expand ourselves to consider other ways of being and other viewpoints, the more we begin to experience our own inner happiness. This happiness is who we really are. It is at the core of our being. One way we can experience this as our true center is to see everything, including our bodies, as objects.

In the following two-part exercise, you'll be expanding your experience of your inner self even further. This exercise will give you a new perspective on who you are, along with a feeling of elation. Give yourself at least five minutes for each part of the exercise.

Inner Focus: Expanding Your Inner Space
Sitting comfortably with your eyes closed, take a few deep breaths to center yourself using the expanded breathing technique you learned in chapter 2 (pages 27–28). Open your eyes and look at your arms and legs and as much of your body as you're able to see as objects. See them as something other

than you. See them in the same context as you see the table, the book, a lamp, or any other object. Sit quietly and don't move your body. Concentrate on not being your body for five minutes.

The conscious you that looked out and saw your body as an object is in fact who *you* really are. That conscious you, independent of surroundings and independent even of your own body is *you*.

With this awareness, repeat the meditation. As you begin to really see your body as an object, you will become aware of an energy pulsating within you.

Close your eyes and turn your focus from your body to that energy inside you. As you focus on that energy, repeat I AM. This is your I AM energy. Stay with that energy for ten minutes, repeating I AM silently to yourself. You'll find that that energy revitalizes you. That energy is *you*.

When you withdraw your senses from outer objects and focus on that energy inside you, you'll find a place of renewal and happiness. Eventually, you will find you can do this with your eyes open.

The Time Is Now

When we begin to see that our perceptions of the world spring from our past experiences and are influenced by them, we can see how we bring our past with us into the present moment. The present moment is also influenced by the future and our expectations about what could or should happen.

We all have goals (future) and experience (past) that serve as guides and teachers, but if we let these ideas about the world become our only basis for knowing it, we become trapped by our own minds.

Meditation gives us a pure experience of the *now* without

the baggage of our concepts. Enjoying the present moment as fully as possible is one of the benefits of meditation. It gives us a pause, a stopping place where we can become aware of our thoughts, and teaches us how to enjoy the present moment by making us conscious. You may have experienced this earlier in the chapter when you experimented with changing a habit, and found yourself more aware and alive in the present moment instead of operating automatically.

When we become aware of how our thoughts and concepts limit our understanding, we begin to put them aside and enjoy each moment as it arises. Eventually, we can go beyond our thoughts to experience the great wealth of peace and calm within.

Who We Really Are

A friend is committed to living in the moment when she travels. She loves traveling so much she works two jobs until she's saved enough money to globetrot for at least three or four months at a time. While she's working, she carefully plans her itinerary and watches her savings mount up. While traveling, she always has a fabulous time. Even when things go wrong—her luggage is lost, her hotel reservation is accidentally canceled, the food is bad, she's sick, there are monsoons, mosquitoes, or delays in her plans—nothing shakes her up. How does she manage this? "I'm determined to be cheerful," she says. "I don't care what happens, I decide even before I leave that whatever happens is for the best. And so it doesn't matter if I have to spend a few extra days somewhere; that just means I get to know the people better. And if I'm sick, I just know that I must have needed the rest or that something better will be coming soon."

In this way, our friend fully experiences the moment, and since she's so determined to enjoy it, she does! Another friend went on a cruise and returned bitterly disappointed. "My vacation was ruined," she said. "They didn't serve coffee." Her idea of a good time was dependent upon having coffee for breakfast. When there wasn't any coffee, she spent two weeks being miserable and not noticing anything else the trip offered.

What we forget is that our rules for happiness are products of our minds. We decide what ingredients are essential for a good time and a fulfilling life based on our concepts of how things *should* be.

The more we let go of old concepts that keep us from enjoying ourselves, the more open we become to new possibilities. In this way, we can transcend whatever limits our notions of the world have imposed on us. When we expand our minds in this way, it's like taking a deep, full breath. A fresh breeze blows through us, dissolving all of our mental restraints.

One of the best ways to experience complete freedom from all of our limitations is to begin to recognize them. The next step is to recognize that we've put them there and then remove them. It is then possible to expand beyond them. The following exercise will give you a chance to explore the vastness of your own consciousness. Although we're finite bodies, we can experience our infinite energy just by letting go of *all* of our limits, including our bodies. This one is great fun. Take at least ten minutes for this exercise, but if you take longer, that's okay, too.

Mini-Meditation: Expanding into Space
Sitting comfortably, take a few deep breaths to center yourself. Close your eyes and focus on feeling your consciousness inside your body. Become aware of that energy within you. Now feel yourself slowly expanding a foot beyond your body in all directions. Expand your consciousness to fill the room you are in. Now feel yourself expanding beyond the walls of the room until eventually you fill the

entire building. Very slowly, feel yourself expanding to include the street you live on, then the entire block, then the whole town or city, then the state you live in, then the country you live in, and then the planet.

Continue to breathe deeply and regularly with each expansion. Next, expand your consciousness to include all the planets, and then the stars and galaxies. Imagine that you encompass the entire universe. Rest in this expanded state for a few minutes.

Although we live in our physical bodies and have to deal with certain physical realities, this meditation can change your outlook whenever you need to put things into their proper perspective.

Meditation enables you to view the world from a fresh perspective, full of possibilities. Functioning at the level of awareness you create in meditation, you become more and more familiar with your inner space and the freedom it provides. Each of the practice sessions makes it easier and easier to get there!

· 5 ·

The Power of Sound

Sound has many uses in meditation and affects us both mentally and physically. Whether or not we're aware of it, we're surrounded by sound. As you become more aware of sound and its effects on you, it becomes easier to use it as a tool for meditation. Simply stated, sound is vibration. In chapter 3 you discovered that thoughts are very subtle vibrations, which cause ripples in consciousness. These subtle vibrations can also take on the grosser form of words. Words are nothing but sound vibrations. If we put a group of words together, we get sentences; from sentences we get ideas; from ideas we get concepts and suddenly we have a whole universe built on and out of words.

The idea of sound creating the universe is nothing new. In ancient India, the sages said that the universe began with a sound and the sound was OM. The Bible says, "In the beginning there was the Word. And the Word was with God, and the Word *was* God." More recently, scientists have supported sound being at the beginning of the world with their big-bang theory. From one primordial vibration, the entire universe manifested and continues to manifest.

The Power of Words

Words are audible vibrations. Using words we articulate and communicate what we want and how we feel. Words are the basic building blocks of the mind. This highly sophisticated age of communications in which we are currently living could not have come about without words. Every culture, from the most primitive to the most civilized communicates through words. Even sign language is a way of expressing words. Words are not only the building blocks of the mind, they're the building blocks of the entire world. They create social structures as well as physical structures, governments as well as the buildings governments are housed in. Words can create a government and also cause it to fall. To quote writer Leo Rosten, "One word can start a war."

What Words Tell Us

One of the first things we encounter when we make our debut on earth is words. They tell us who we are, what we are like, how to see ourselves, how to see the world; they tell us if we're bad, they tell us if we're good.

By the time we get to school, we're already reacting to ourselves as being a particular way because of the words that have been directed toward us. We then behave the way we believe ourselves to be, causing other people to react to us in that way. Very soon the way we believe ourselves to be is who we become and we don't realize we can be any other way. If our parents tell us we're smart, we become smart; if they tell us we're clumsy, we become clumsy; if they tell us we're beautiful, even if by normal standards we aren't beautiful, we become beautiful by our actions and the way we carry and see ourselves.

Each of us experiences words differently. Some words annoy us while others make us feel good. Many people have a favorite word or expression that they use more often than any other. Some words have more of an impact on us than others. We all have certain words or expressions that carry special meaning for us. They may reflect our childhood or a relationship or how we feel about ourselves.

Sound in the form of words can create concepts in our minds that keep us from connecting with our inner energy. Words can pull us off center, and anything that disturbs our minds in this way disturbs our ability to meditate. That's why it's important to take a closer look at how words affect you.

In this next exercise, you'll explore which words have the most powerful effects on you. You'll need your notebook for this one.

Outer Focus: How Words Affect Us
Take all the time you need to make two lists of words. List A should contain words or phrases that make you feel good, for example, "You're so thoughtful, generous, and handsome." List B should contain words and phrases that have the opposite effect, for example, "Don't do that again! Can't you smile? You're so stupid! What's wrong with you?"

Once you've made your lists, read them through again. Are you surprised by the words that appear on your lists? Look at the words once more and write down the kind of reaction each word causes in you. Happy. Angry. Annoyed. Shocked. Insecure. Really give it some thought. Are you surprised by your reactions?

You may also want to add the tone of voice in which something is said: harsh, accusing, loving, kidding. Contemplate why you are affected the way you are. Save these lists for future reference. You may find that as you go through the different exercises in this book, the words on your lists will affect you differently. For now, however, just making your lists has made you more aware of the power of the word.

❦

What Words Can Do

As kids, whenever we were taunted with name calling, or other kids hurled insults at us, the reply was almost invariably, "Sticks and stones may break my bones, but names can never hurt me." As it turns out, words can cause infinitely more damage.

We're continually subjected to words. Words on TV, radio, in the newspapers, and words from all the people around us. Words tell us how to do this, how to do that, how to think, and what to think. They can even make us sick. Just as positive affirmations and audiotapes can program us toward healthier mental and physical habits, we can also be negatively programmed. How many times have you listened to TV commercials that told you "When you have a headache, buy . . ." or "When you're sick in bed with the flu, buy such and such a product." Not *if* you have a headache, or *if* you're sick in bed with the flu. The word "when" suggests that you *will* have a headache, you *will* be sick with the flu. If you do become sick, the words and products are already implanted in your mind. And of course, aspirin and other over-the-counter drug sales continue to increase because we're very suggestible.

When listening to TV commercials that implant negative suggestions, counteract them with the word "erase." Just repeat "erase" to yourself when you hear anything that tells you that you will be sick or gives you any other negative suggestion. Be vigilant. Just this kind of awareness blocks the negativity from automatically entering your consciousness.

You can also use the erase technique to clear your mind of thoughts when practicing meditation. In fact, try it right now.

Inner Focus: Clearing the Mind
Sitting comfortably with your back straight, take a few deep breaths to center yourself. With your eyes closed visu-

alize a blank blackboard in your mind and focus on it. Each time a thought arises, see yourself erasing it with a blackboard eraser, using broad sweeping strokes. Each time the blackboard is erased, become familiar with the clear space you've created. Rest in it for as long as possible, experiencing the peace found here.

Repeat this exercise for five minutes.

Did you notice that when words appeared they moved you away from this space? Did a thought arise that made you want to get up and do something else, like make a phone call or eat something? As you've just experienced, in words we find the subtle beginnings of all of the actions we take.

Beyond Words

The meaning of a word is often colored by the tone in which it is spoken. The subtlety of the sound in which words are couched can have a tremendous influence on how we perceive the words spoken to us.

Sometimes, when we speak, others hear something in our voice that we're not aware is there. The tone of the words spoken sometimes projects the underlying feeling, which may be at odds with what we're actually saying. As a result, people respond to our tone rather than to the content. Unless we become more aware of how we sound, we can have difficulties in communicating with others. You can test yourself by listening to yourself as you speak.

Let's try this experiment. Choose a word, any word. Say it out loud. Say it as fast as you can. Say it as slowly as you can, enunciating each syllable. Say it softly, say it loudly. Say it like you mean it. Say it lovingly, say it angrily. Laugh as you say it. Sing it high, sing it low.

As you can see, one simple word can have many nuances.

If someone says, "I love you," you feel all warm and loving. If someone says, "I hate you," you feel terrible. Many times people say one thing and mean another. The more attuned to the nuances of sound we become, the more able we are to hear the underlying meaning of the words; the subtle vibrations that tell the truth about what is being said.

An excellent illustration of how sound belies the word is found in a Zen tale in which a blind man living near a Zen temple spends his days listening to people as they pass his home.

Over the years, having only his ears to rely on, he became sensitive to the tone underlying people's words. Day after day, he would listen to their endless gossip and in this way he learned to differentiate between what was true and what was untrue by the tone in which words were exchanged. He noticed that when people expressed happiness at someone else's good news, there was always a tinge of jealousy. If they expressed sorrow at another's misfortune, he could always detect a hint of pleasure. In all his years of listening, he heard only one voice in which the words and tone matched, and that was the voice of the temple master. Of him he said, "When he expressed happiness, there was nothing but happiness in his voice. When he expressed sorrow, there was only sorrow in his voice."

As we become more aware through meditation, our words and the tone of our words come into alignment, reflecting the "at oneness" with the purity of the inner state.

The World of Vibration

Words aren't the only sound vibrations that affect us. We're surrounded by all kinds of vibrations, whether or not we're aware of them. Our moods are often affected by the background sounds in our environment. Some sounds—birds singing, a waterfall or bubbling brook, the distant bass of a foghorn, laughter—are pleasant and welcome, and make you feel happy inside, while others—jackhammers, screeching subway trains, and car horns—are unwelcome irritants.

Some sounds are almost universally irritating, like chalk squeaking on a blackboard or a fork on a frying pan. These vibrations can create physical reactions: chills down the spine, goosebumps, or gritted teeth.

Sound vibrations are so powerful, they can cause incredible destruction. Sound can shatter glass; sound is said to have tumbled the walls of Jericho, and when soldiers march across a bridge in column formation they always break stride to keep the bridge from entering into a state of vibration that could cause the bridge to collapse.

We're so enmeshed in a web of sound all the time, we tend to push all the different kinds of sounds out of our consciousness, especially those of us who live in big cities or highly populated suburban areas, where noise pollution is a major stress producer. Tuning out sound is a built-in survival technique since there's only so much sensory input we can handle at any one time. Yet these sounds are still entering our consciousness.

As we begin to focus on the different sounds we're surrounded with, we find an amazing variety that we tune out. Sit quietly for a moment and listen. You'll need your notebook for this one.

Outer Focus: Listening to the World Around Us

List all of the sounds around you in your notebook. Everything from the chirping of a bird, to the sound of the TV, to the wind blowing through the trees, to the howl of the coyote, a car passing by on the road, an airplane flying overhead, the oil burner going on and off, the air conditioner whirring. Just jot down every sound you hear. There will be sounds that you didn't even realize were there.

When you think you've noted every sound around you, down to the sound of your pen or pencil on the paper, listen still harder. Is there anything new that comes into your awareness? Very often there are underlying vibrations and hums from refrigerators and other electrical equipment that are so much a part of your environment, you no longer hear them. Are you missing these sounds on your list? Do they exist in your environment? Are you surprised by how much peripheral sound surrounds you? Becoming aware of sound is another way of recognizing the impact that the outer world has on us.

You can then use these sounds to go deeper into your inner world. In this next exercise, you're going to be using the sounds in your immediate environment to draw you into meditation.

Inner Focus: Following a Sound into Silence

Sitting comfortably, with your back straight, take a few deep breaths to center yourself. With your eyes closed, listen to the sounds around you once again. Pick one specific sound and focus all of your awareness on it. Really try to merge into that sound; become one with the sound.

As you merge into the sound, you'll be merging into your own silence. If thoughts distract you, just refocus on the sound. Give yourself ten minutes with this exercise.

When you open your eyes, be aware of the difference between your inner and outer state. You'll find yourself feeling quite refreshed.

In Tune with the Universe

For centuries philosophers and mystics have spoken about "the symphony of the spheres." It's said that if we had the receiving power to tune into the sound emanations of the universe, the planets, and the stars, we would hear harmonious music.

Everything vibrates at its own frequency, so you can imagine that if all of nature's subtle vibrations became audible, we would hear an incredible symphony.

As part of the universe, the human body, too, has its unique vibration. Our blood vibrates and so do our muscles. Different cells in our bodies vibrate at different rates of speed. The vibrations made by particular sounds set up sympathetic vibrations in our physical bodies. In other words, we resonate to the sounds around us.

There are several systems in the body that are particularly sensitive to sound vibrations. Every human being has seven nerve plexuses. Each plexus is a network of nerve ganglia which distributes the nerves to specific areas of the body. These centers are very powerful and sensitive. They are located right below the chest (the solar plexus), at the top of the head, beneath the brain, in the throat, the heart, the reproductive region, and the anal region. In the same locations we find the endocrine glands which secrete hormones regulating growth, reproduction, metabolism, and other chemical processes of the body. Both physical systems are energized by subtle energy centers called "chakras." The chakras are associated with specific vibrations that bring the body into balance through their effect on the endocrine and nervous systems.

Sound vibrations are used in several current therapeutic practices, such as chiropractics, to release muscle tension. Healers who work with sound believe that each body harmonizes with different vibrations. Vibrations that are in harmony with the body encourage natural healing while others may cause irritation and illness.

Music Has Charms

In ancient India, music was an important remedy for disease. Instruments like the tamboura, a beautiful long-necked string instrument, and the ektara, a one-stringed instrument, were found to have a beneficial effect on people who were ill. The sounds emanating from them were said to bring the chakras into harmonious vibration. To this day in India, these instruments are used both for their beautiful sounds and the effects of these sounds on the chakras.

A powerful way to harmonize with this inner vibration is through singing. When we sing our bodies become the instruments through which sound vibrates. In the same way that the body of a guitar is a resonating chamber for the sound caused by strumming the strings, our head and chest are resonating chambers for our vocal chords.

Singing has been used in various religious traditions to both uplift the heart and still the mind. Gregorian chants, hymns, and spirituals are part of the Christian tradition, in Judaism congregational singing is an integral part of the service, and chanting is an essential part of the Hindu and Buddhist paths. As we chant or sing hymns, a beneficial vibration takes place within our bodies while the words speak to our hearts, and we find ourselves feeling very good.

If you attend a church, temple, or synagogue, you may already be aware of the effect religious music has on you. Classical music, too, puts the listener in a peaceful state, and heavy-metal music agitates the listener. It would be very unusual for upheaval to take place among the audience at a Bach concert, whereas violent behavior demonstrated by the destruction of instruments and harm to performers and audience members has taken place at some rock or heavy-metal concerts. If we examine the nature of these sounds and combinations of sounds more closely, we find that the music that causes restlessness and violence stimulates the lower chakras, which are associated with the grosser and more primitive areas of human development, while the sounds that stimulate the upper chakras associated with higher consciousness and spirituality, create great peace and exaltation.

You can experience the power of music yourself by doing the following exercise.

Outer Focus: From Rap to Rhapsody

Turn on the radio and listen to at least two selections of three different kinds of music. Choose from classical, mellow, heavy metal, country, pop, jazz, or religious music. Listen carefully to each type of music. Notice where in your body you feel a response. Head, heart, stomach?

Write down the feelings each type of music evokes in you and the type of thoughts each kind of music creates.

As you begin to become aware of the effects sound has on you, you tune into your environment in a whole new way. The more aware you become of outside stimuli, the more you appreciate the silence within.

A New Realm of Sound

When you begin to realize how powerful sound is, how powerful words are, then you begin to realize how powerful silence is. It's in silence that we go to the place where sound originates. It's in silence that we begin to go deeper and deeper into that inner storehouse of joy.

Since we're surrounded by sound, we're often unaware of how many sound vibrations *we* create as we go through the day. In the next exercise, you'll experience a greater awareness of sound by focusing your attention on the vibrations *you* set into motion.

For instance, did you ever notice that some people walk like stampeding elephants while others shuffle along? Have you been able to recognize certain people by the sound of their footsteps? Have you ever listened to your eating sounds? The fork hitting the plate? Slurping, crunching? What kind of sounds are you making when you eat? Did you ever listen as you poured liquid into a glass or cup? When you read do you turn the pages of a newspaper like a clap of thunder or do you do it quietly? Some people even breathe heavily. Do you slam doors or quietly click them closed?

Outer Focus: A Waking Meditation

For the next twenty-four hours try to be aware of the sounds you make. As you go through the day, focus on doing everything as silently as possible. Focus on the silence of each action. By focusing on the silence of your actions, you will become aligned with your own silence and experience the power of meditation in your waking state.

Silence has its own sound. The more you listen for it, the more in touch you'll become with the deep inner peace that will begin to permeate your entire life.

The sound of silence is the sound of our inner joy. When we speak of silence in this way, we're not only talking about silence as opposed to outside sounds, we're talking about silence as opposed to the mental tapes that repeat themselves in our minds—the worries, concepts, and other inner dialogues we've discussed that keep us from experiencing the black velvet sound of deep inner silence.

To give our sensory and nervous systems a rest, it's essential for us to turn to our own silence. The following exercise will take you deep into a new realm of silence if you sit very quietly and listen very intently.

Inner Focus: The Sounds of Silence

Sitting comfortably with your eyes closed, take a few deep breaths to center yourself. Imagine a snowflake falling on a bed of snow. Listen very hard for the sound it makes. Or a rose petal sailing to the ground. Again listen to the sound. Listen to a star as it twinkles or a bud as it unfolds. Can you hear a blade of grass coming up through a crack in the sidewalk? Listen to any one of these sounds inside yourself in silence. If you listen hard enough, you will hear the silence of your own heart. This silence is very deep, very enveloping, and very full of love.

Magic Words: Mantras

Surprisingly enough, words can also bring us in synch with our inner silence. In the same way that they take us away from that inner joy, they can bring us back to that state. There are special words called "mantras" that silence the mind. Mantras came from ancient sages who were merged with that inner silence and have been used as the key to meditation ever since. These words are the sound vibrations of the inner self, and, when repeated, they set up sympathetic vibrations inside us that draw us into the silence of this inner state. Our minds become still and we become completely attuned to our inner joy.

OM is one of these sounds. It is a mantra that made its appearance in the West in a big way in the 1960s, but has been chanted by great masters since the beginning of time. The mantra OM rhymes with home, and it takes you to that home in the heart where a treasure trove of joy and happiness await you. When we reach this place we recognize it as the place we have been looking for all along. Just by repeating this syllable, you begin to experience the power of its vibration. The more you repeat it and the longer you hold it, the stronger the effect. It creates a high alpha state in which you will feel euphoric and energized, yet relaxed.

Mini-Meditation: OM Sweet OM

Sitting comfortably with your eyes closed, take a few deep breaths to center yourself. Slowly repeat OM out loud. Let the sound begin at the level of the abdomen, then feel it rise up to the heart. Feel the vibration of the O sound at the heart level. When the MMM wants to come out, let it resonate through your nasal chambers. As you hold the MMM, feel the vibration at the top of your head. Repeat the sound, letting it resonate within you. Feel its vibration in the heart and head. Let it create warmth in the heart area. Hold the sound as long as possible. Repeat OM as you breathe in and OM as you breathe out. Do this for a full five minutes. How does it make you feel?

You can also repeat OM silently to yourself any time your mind becomes agitated or cluttered with thoughts. By focusing on the syllable OM instead of your thoughts, it will take you to the place of stillness inside.

When we reach a point where we can rest contentedly in the heart in the middle of all sounds, we know we've come home. As we continue repeating OM, letting its vibrations fill us, we get closer and closer to our inner peace and joy.

• 6 •

The Mind/Body Connection

The power of our thoughts is not only strong enough to intrude on our naturally peaceful mental state, it can have far-reaching physical effects, too. In doing the inner and outer focus exercises, with your thoughts centered on loved ones or pleasant experiences, you may have experienced a surge of joy or a feeling of well-being in your physical body. Your mind actually triggered bodily sensations. More dramatic examples of the mind's effect on the body include the rush of adrenalin you experience when you get angry or excited, or when, at the thought of a favorite food, you begin to salivate.

Just as our minds affect our bodies, meditation can have an effect as well. When we still the mind through meditation, our bodies relax. As we become aware of the effect our minds have on our bodies, we can begin to use certain techniques, like meditation, not only to heal the body but to keep it healthy.

Our minds have such a powerful influence over us that they affect even the automatic, self-regulating chemical processes like the flow of hormones. This link between our thoughts and our bodies is so strong that a mere thought can evoke a powerful chemical response. For example, if we think we see a snake, it doesn't matter if it really *is* a snake or if we just *think* it is, our body reacts the same way, with a powerful chemical reaction known as the fight or flight response.

This life-saving response is a reaction to the threat of bodily harm. When our ancestors were faced with a saber-toothed tiger or a giant mastodon, the fight or flight response mobilized the body within seconds. Their minds registered danger and they reacted. Adrenalin was pumped into the blood, heart rate and blood pressure increased, the breathing rate increased, metabolism was faster, and there was an increase in the blood flow to the muscles. The body was ready! Fight or flee!

That same response operates in exactly the same way in modern man. The body's rapid mobilization in response to danger still occurs, but it also functions in response to other challenges. Instead of running from a saber-toothed tiger the way our ancestors did, we're the football quarterback headed for the goal posts. In place of the hunt, we're after that big promotion or trying to catch the 5:15 P.M. train home.

In primitive times the fight or flight response was activated for short periods and then released by action, but today, this response is constantly stimulated due to stress.

Ready for Action

Stress actively elicits the fight or flight response, with the same result—hormones like adrenalin or cortisol are pumped into our systems, blood pressure rises, heart rate increases. The body mobilizes itself to meet the challenge of this new external demand. However, without the physical release of brute combat or running for our lives, the hormones which have been dumped into our bloodstream just sit there, our muscles contract, our whole body is mobilized for action—but there is no release. Here's an example of what happens:

You are having an argument with your boss, spouse,

lover, parent, best friend, client, or colleague. It doesn't matter who's wrong or right, the chemical response is the same. The adrenalin begins to flow, your heart beats faster, blood pressure rises, breathing patterns change. Physically, in the space of a few minutes, your body chemistry has dramatically transformed. Fight? Flight? Of course not. Instead, the muscles contract, your shoulder blades inch toward each other, your neck muscles constrict.

The negative emotions experienced during stress drain energy from us. After a stress response, you may experience a sense of physical exhaustion. But, instead of releasing all of that energy in a physical explosion—that is, running away or disarming the enemy—all of that energy implodes right inside you. The anger and upset remain with you, reinforced by the mind and held in by the body. Later, every time your mind recalls the incident, your body reacts again and again to the same stimulus. Even though the provocative incident may be days, weeks, or even months in the past our attachment to the event, both mentally and physically, remains.

If those angry feelings aren't dealt with, you may vent some of that excess adrenalin energy by railing at someone else or by yelling back at the boss. But even that doesn't help because your mind keeps your body at that same fever pitch.

As a result, we suffer from a variety of anxieties and their related symptoms. Unresolved, these symptoms can lead to headaches, backaches, allergies, arthritis, asthma, insomnia, skin disorders, colitis, ulcers, sexual problems, diarrhea, canker sores, hypertension, and heart disease.

How can we acknowledge and then release these negative emotions? One way is by dealing with them immediately. A very simple exercise which helps release any negative emotions you may have after a stress reaction is one that actually lets you visualize the energy of the emotion itself. The next time you feel upset or angry, try the following exercise.

Special Focus: Releasing the Inner Storm

Sit quietly for a moment and close your eyes. Focus on the energy of what you're feeling rather than what caused the feeling. Be aware of how this affects you physically. Now take the energy of what you're feeling and visualize it as a natural force. Imagine a hurricane out at sea or a tornado raging across a barren plain. Focus all of the energy of what you're feeling into the hurricane. Become one with this natural force. Allow it to play out as it does in nature.

Do this for five to ten minutes, until you feel your anger dissipating. Now watch as the storm blows away from you.

Rest in the calm after the storm.

Stress Is How You See It

Stress can certainly be at the root of many of our health problems, but in recent years it has become the scapegoat of our culture. It is blamed for diseases like cancer and hypertension and considered one of the causes of drug and alcohol abuse. But stress is also a natural response to external demands. Normal stress is what keeps life exciting and challenging. New studies have even shown that normal stress levels can stimulate the immune system instead of suppressing it.

Stress can be a positive factor, giving us the edge we need to perform at our peak. Examples of positive stress might include the challenge of a new job, beginning college, getting married, or performing on stage for the first time.

The difference between positive and negative stress has a great deal to do with our own perceptions of it. What one person sees as an exciting challenge might be seen by someone else as a burden or a threat.

Some personality types are more likely to become stressed than others. Those who exhibit hostility and pessimism are more likely to suffer the adverse effects of stress. Those who are able to take a more philosophical approach to life's events are less susceptible to the harmful effects of stress.

How affected are you by everyday stress? Take a look at the list below and consider each question.

Outer Focus: Stress Test

Do you do more than one thing at once?
Do you often lose your temper?
Are you always in a hurry?
Do you like to do things as fast as possible?
Do you find it difficult to leave the office behind?
Do you feel guilty when you're not doing something?
Do you find that you don't make time for yourself?
Do you suffer from insomnia?
Do you find yourself worrying about everything?
Do you like to be in control of things?
Are you often annoyed by inconsiderate and selfish people?
Are you usually the one who does the job best?

If you found yourself answering yes to many of the questions, you probably experience some level of stress on a daily basis.

Each of us perceives the world in our own way. Some people are "B types," able to go through life without letting much of anything bother them. They're able to shrug off daily annoyances and let them go. "A types" are frequently upset and have a tendency to critically evaluate their own performance and the performances of those around them. Most people fall somewhere in the middle, but we all have something that "pushes our buttons."

Responding to Stress

One of the most common reactions to stressful situations is a change in breathing pattern. You may have found yourself holding your breath or breathing very shallowly when you're in a stressful situation. This type of breathing affects you both mentally and physically. The breath not only brings oxygen into the system, carrying vital energy to every cell in the body, it also carries waste products like carbon dioxide out of the system. Shallow breathing, then, not only reduces the amount of oxygen to vital organs like the brain, but it allows toxins and waste to remain in the bloodstream.

In a stressful situation, remembering to breath properly can have a significant effect on the whole body. By really filling the lungs and breathing calmly for a few minutes, more oxygen gets to the brain and muscles, more toxins are eliminated from your system, and tense muscles begin to relax. The heart responds by beating in rhythm with your slow and steady breathing. A calmer heart will make you mentally calmer and better able to deal with whatever crisis is at hand.

The next time you find yourself in a stressful situation, focus on your breathing. Are you holding your breath or taking short, shallow breaths? Consciously begin to take deeper, slower breaths. Over the next several days, become aware of how you breathe in different situations. How are you breathing right now?

This next exercise combines a good focal point for the mind with a deep breathing technique that increases oxygen flow and relaxes the body. Although it is similar to the expanded breathing exercise you learned in chapter 2, this is an excellent technique to use when you are feeling upset or are having difficulty centering yourself for meditation.

Let's practice taking a deeper breath. Spend five minutes on this exercise.

Inner Focus: Taking a Breather
Sitting comfortably, breathe in through your nose counting slowly to four, five, or six. Feel your rib cage expand. Your abdomen should protrude slightly on the inhalation. Exhale

slowly through the nose, doubling the number you counted to on the inhalation. So, for example, if you inhaled to the count of six, exhale to the count of twelve. Let the air slowly fill your lungs as you inhale and exhale as gently as possible. Don't force the air. Do this for one minute.

Become aware of how you feel. Calmer? More relaxed?

You can use any of the breathing techniques you've learned to center yourself before meditation. Or you may want to try a breathing technique in moments of high-level stress. Taking deep, slow, even breaths can reenergize and relax you and have an overall positive effect on your emotional as well as your physical state.

Lightening Up

Laughter also helps us take deeper breaths. A good belly laugh can do wonders for muscle tension, too. It massages deep muscles that may never be reached otherwise and it improves circulation around vital organs. Scientists have found that laughter increases breathing and oxygen exchange and it may stimulate the body to produce endorphins, the body's natural pain killers.

Research has also shown that facial muscles can affect the emotions, so that just by smiling, you can improve your outlook and lift your spirits. The following exercise is a great way to release tension. You may want to try it when you're in the middle of a tense situation, a situation where smiling is the last thing you would naturally do. Even just *imagining* yourself smiling can help.

Using this exercise, we've found that we wound up laughing at how seriously we were taking incidents that didn't merit that kind of energy. Just by laughing, our perceptions automatically changed, making it much easier to deal with stressful situations. Try it for yourself right now.

Special Focus: Get Happy

Sitting quietly, begin to smile. Feel the corners of your mouth rise. It doesn't matter what you're thinking about. Concentrate on the feeling as your lips curl upward. As you smile, can you feel laughter welling up inside? Try to concentrate on where the feeling is coming from. Allow this feeling to course through your entire body. Stay with this awareness for several minutes.

Releasing Tension

Our minds suffer when we experience stress, but so do our bodies. The accumulated tensions of the day, the week, and often a lifetime remain with us, becoming so ingrained that we hardly notice them. The results can be far reaching: We carry one shoulder a little higher than the other, or we slouch a bit, or lean to one side, or our head sags a little. As we age, these physical postures become habitual. Muscular contractions, too often repeated and never fully released, become permanent constrictions, a reflection of our mental and emotional habits. Although we become, in effect, "bent out of shape," we hardly even notice the change.

When our muscles are contracted in this way, our breathing can become chronically shallow, reducing the flow of oxygen to the brain. These same contractions can affect our blood pressure, too, causing it to remain chronically higher than normal.

An early attempt at exploring how the mind can influence the body was biofeedback. People hooked up to an electrocardiogram and various other monitoring devices, focused their thoughts on changing their heart rate, for example. It was found that using this mental focus people could either increase or decrease their heartbeat. Without being hooked up to a machine, we can still utilize the mind's ability to influence the body by meditating and focusing our awareness.

Just as the fight or flight response is a lifesaving reaction, mobilizing the body for action when faced with physical danger, we also have a mechanism for dealing with too much stress. This response slows our heart rate, decreases blood pressure, and releases muscle tension at its very deepest levels.

Studies have shown that the best way to elicit this "relaxation response" is through meditation. Meditation has been known to decrease stress hormone levels in the bloodstream as well as decrease the biological age of practitioners. It can also increase pain threshold levels and dramatically change our brain-wave patterns.

Meditation has been used to balance physical, spiritual, and mental energies for centuries. What the ancient saints and sages knew and practiced has been finding its way into the popular culture and the healing professions ever since. Modern scientists are discovering that meditation can balance body chemistry and penetrate the deep muscles, and has even been shown to have a beneficial effect on the entire nervous system.

In the next exercise, you will be using meditation to help you release some of your muscular tensions. Read through the exercise before beginning. Familiarize yourself with it so you don't have to refer to the book. You may want to have someone read the exercise aloud, guiding you through the relaxation of different parts of the body, or you may want to record it.

Mini-Meditation: Complete Physical Relaxation
Find a quiet place where you can lie down undisturbed. Lie comfortably on your back, with your hands resting palm up a few inches from your sides, legs about shoulder width apart. Take a few deep breaths to center yourself.

Begin by stretching and tensing the right leg. Tense all the muscles in your foot, leg, and thigh and raise your leg two inches off the ground, holding it up for five seconds.

Drop the leg, roll it back and forth, then forget about it. Repeat this for the left leg. Stretch it out, tense all the muscles, lift it two inches off the ground for five seconds, drop it, roll it back and forth, then forget about it.

Stretch out your right arm all the way through your hand and fingers, your fingers splayed. With your arm tensed, make a fist with your hand and raise your arm and hand two inches off the ground. Hold it for five seconds then let it drop and roll it from side to side, then forget about it. Repeat for the left arm. Stretch it out, through the hands, splaying the fingers, tensing all the muscles. Make your hand into a fist, raise the arm two inches off the ground, hold for five seconds, then drop the arm, roll it from side to side, and forget about it.

Tense the buttocks. Really tense them as tightly as you can, then release.

Inhaling through the nostrils, slowly take a deep full breath, drawing it all the way down into the abdomen. Feel the abdomen puffing out like a balloon. When you feel you've taken in all the breath you can, hold it for five seconds, then open the mouth wide and let the breath rush out.

Inhaling through the nostrils, slowly take a deep full breath, drawing it down into the chest area. Feel the chest pushing all the way out. When you feel you've taken in all the breath you can, take in one tiny bit more, hold it for five seconds, then open the mouth and let the breath rush out.

Keeping your arms on the floor, move your shoulders up off the floor toward the chest, hold for five seconds, then let them go. Then, with your arms still on the floor, move your shoulders up toward your ears, hold for five seconds, then let them go. Then, arms still on the floor, move your shoulders down toward your legs, hold for five seconds and let go.

Very gently and slowly, roll your head to the right, as if

someone were cradling it in their hands and moving it for you. Roll it as far right as you can without creating any tension in the neck. Hold for five seconds. Just as gently and slowly, roll the head back to center. Now gently and slowly roll the head to the left as far as you can without tensing the neck. Hold for five seconds, and slowly roll the head back to center.

Stretch the face, eyes wide open looking up, mouth wide open, tongue out. Hold for five seconds then relax. Suck in the cheeks, hold for five seconds then relax. Scrunch the whole face up, eyes squeezed shut, mouth squeezed shut, everything scrunched up toward the nose. Hold for five seconds then release.

Now, without moving anything, check your body from toe to head to see if there's any place where you might still have tension.

Starting with the toes on both feet, check to see that they're completely relaxed. Check your ankles, legs, knees, and thighs. Feel the relaxation deep within the muscles. Feel your buttocks relaxed, sinking into the floor. Feel your pelvic region completely relaxed. Feel relaxation penetrating deeply into the abdomen, through to the back. Feel your chest totally relaxed. Feel relaxation in all your back muscles. Feel the relaxation in your arms all the way down through the fingertips. Feel your shoulders relaxed. Feel your neck and head completely relaxed. Rest in this position for as long as you like.

Through meditation, we're able to tap into the body's own vast resources for coping with physical and emotional stress, as well as its capacity for healing. Just as we learned that we are not our minds, in the same way, we are not our bodies.

It has been said that the whole is greater than the sum of

its parts. In this same way, we are greater than the sum total of these two aspects of ourselves—mind and body. Meditation allows us to utilize that greater whole.

Once we begin to tap this inner reservoir, we can begin to feel healthier and function in a more productive way.

° 7 °

Daily Meditation

Now that you're familiar with the basics of meditation, you're ready to begin daily practice. The four-week program that follows is designed to expand upon the inner and outer focus techniques and mini-meditations you've done throughout the book.

Over the next four weeks, you'll experience a variety of meditations that will deepen your experience; some are ancient and some are new. They are arranged in a specific sequence which allows you to build on what you've practiced in previous days and weeks. You'll also be increasing your length of time in meditation from fifteen minutes to a half hour by adding five minutes to your practice each week.

You'll find that as you honor the meditative energy by meditating every day, it honors you. As with any type of exercise, the more you practice the better the results. If you practice for a full month, you'll see changes taking place in your reactions to life that make the world seem lighter and your life more joyous. Your commitment is an integral part of the program.

Keep in mind that meditation is different for everyone. Approach it with an open mind and let it unfold as it will. Set aside any expectations of how your meditation should be. Merely focusing the mind on one thing will release a relaxation response and bring results for you.

Remember that meditation is a dynamic experience therefore your experience of it won't always be the same. Some days will be ecstatic and joyous, while at other times you may feel blocked or you may find your mind filled with thoughts. Try to go beyond the emotions that this may provoke. As thoughts come up in meditation—and they will—just watch them float away or dissolve. The important thing is not to get involved with them and to always bring your mind back to the meditation technique.

Try to be patient with yourself and not judge your meditations. Simply observe your reactions and which meditations work best for you. There is no competition here, not even with yourself, nor are there any hard and fast rules. This is your safe place. Meditation is a haven, a refuge from the chaos of the world. It is a gift you give yourself. Enjoy it.

When to Meditate

One of the first things to decide when beginning a meditation program is the time of day that's most convenient for you.

Traditionally, morning meditation is preferred because it centers you for whatever comes your way during the course of the day. It's also a good time because you're still relaxed from a night's sleep.

However, evening practice also has its advantages if morning meditation isn't feasible for you. Meditating in the evening refreshes you after a long day's work, and may either perk you up for an evening's activity, or relax you for a good night's sleep.

Whatever time you choose, whether it's first thing in the morning before breakfast, in the evening after work, or at night before bedtime, it's a good idea to be consistent. By meditating at the same time every day, your mind and body hunger for meditation in the same way that your stomach becomes hungry for food at mealtimes. Since we're creatures of habit, setting up a pattern like this will make meditation easier.

Where to Practice

In the same way that it's most effective to meditate at the same time every day, we recommend that you set aside a particular place for your meditation. Choose a place that is not trafficked by other people. Your space should be reserved solely for meditation. However, if a totally private space is not available, don't worry; merely practicing in the same place all the time will build up an energy in that space that will draw you into meditation. Not only will particles of that energy permeate the space you meditate in, they will also permeate the clothing you wear. For this reason, we suggest that you wear the same clothing each time you meditate. Use a special set of clothes for meditation only—maybe a sweatsuit, or some other loose-fitting clothing that doesn't cut you around the waist or bind you in any way. Shoes are removed for meditation both for comfort and to keep your space clear of any street vibrations.

How to Prepare

There are several ways in which you can prepare yourself and at the same time make your mind more receptive to meditation. For instance, lighting a candle or burning incense has a very calming effect. These acts have long been associated with purifying the atmosphere, but they also help to quiet the mind. As you light the candle and the incense, you're already beginning to slow down from your day and to create an atmosphere of peace. Using incense or candles makes meditation a very special occasion, one that you begin to look forward to as "your time."

Posture

An important element in meditation is posture. The recommended posture is sitting in a comfortable cross-legged position on a cushion, a folded-up blanket, or anything that elevates you at least two inches off the floor. This allows your legs and hip joints to relax without being scrunched into the pelvis. Your back should be straight, your hands on your knees either palms up or palms down. If you like, you can rest your hands palms up on your knees with the thumb and forefinger joined in a circle. This is said to lock the energy into your body. An alternate hand position is resting the hands palms up in the lap, the right hand cradled in the left. You can also join the thumb and forefinger of each hand together in this position, if you wish.

Since it is most comfortable to have some back support in

this position, you may want to sit against a wall. If your legs become uncomfortable in this position, alternative postures include sitting with your back against a wall with your knees brought up to your chest, feet flat on the floor, or you can stretch your legs out in front of you. In either position, you can rest your hands on your knees or in your lap.

If you can't sit on the floor, use a straight-backed chair. Sit with your back straight, your feet flat on the floor. Here, too, you may rest your hands on your knees with your thumb and forefinger joined in a circle, or use any of the hand positions mentioned above.

Another position that can be used for meditation is one in which you lie flat on your back, your arms a few inches from your sides, legs about shoulder width apart. In hatha yoga, this is known as the corpse position. It's one in which the body finds its natural resting place. You experienced this in chapter 6 when you relaxed all the muscles in your body.

In this posture, hands are palms up, and as in the first and second posture, you can join your thumb and forefinger together in a circle if you like. One of the reasons this position isn't highly recommended is because it often leads to sleep instead of meditation.

The one material investment we strongly recommend in conjunction with meditation is a timer, if you don't already have one. This relieves your mind from having to worry about how long you've been meditating. Those of you who cook can borrow the kitchen timer; many digital watches have built-in alarms that are excellent for this purpose, too.

The Breath

In meditation, the breath is spoken of as the vehicle of meditation. It is the bridge between the conscious and unconscious mind. If we focus on the breath with our conscious awareness, the outer world recedes into the background of our consciousness and we're able to fall into meditation more easily.

Focusing on the breath is one effective way to reach that inner place of peace and joy. You may have experienced this when you practiced the focusing techniques that used breathing.

Before you begin your daily meditation, we suggest that you center yourself by taking a few deep breaths using a three-part hatha yoga breathing technique. This deep breathing exercise is an excellent preparation for meditation.

Although this is called the "three-part breathing technique," it is merely broken down into three parts for learning. The real aim is to make each three-part breath one long, smoothly flowing deep breath, beginning at the abdomen, moving up through the lower rib-cage area, and finally up under the collar bones. When we breathe in this way, our lungs take in seven times more oxygen than we normally do. This eliminates many of the toxins the body has accumulated, stimulates blood flow, and relaxes deep muscles.

Taking three deep three-part breaths just before meditation will calm your mind and relax your body just enough to help you glide into meditation.

Three-Part Breathing

Once you're seated or lying down comfortably, inhale through the nose. Slowly draw air all the way down into the abdomen so you feel the abdomen expanding. Hold it for a second, then gently contract the abdomen, slowly pushing the breath up and out through the nose.

Next, inhaling through the nose, again slowly draw the breath down into the abdomen until you feel it expanding. With the abdomen still expanded, continue inhaling into the lower chest so that you feel your rib cage expanding. Then slowly release the breath through the nose by pushing the air out, first from the chest region, and then from the abdomen until the abdomen is slightly contracted.

The third part of the technique adds the upper chest region. Again, we begin by slowly drawing the breath in through the nose, down into the abdomen, gently expanding the abdomen, moving the air up to the chest, gently expanding the lower rib cage, and this time, up through the upper chest so that you feel the expansion of the lungs all the way up to your collar bones. Hold the breath for a second, then exhale through the nose, letting the air out in the same order: releasing the breath first from the abdomen, then the lower chest, and finally, the upper chest.

As you breathe in this way, focus your attention on the air flowing in and then out. Watch as the air fills your diaphragm, then your lungs, bringing oxygen to every part of your body. As you exhale, feel all of your muscle tension disappear. Watching the breath in this way not only ensures that you are doing it properly, it helps to focus your mind in preparation for meditation.

Keeping a Journal

If you've been using a journal or keeping a log during the inner and outer focuses and mini-meditations throughout the book as we suggested, you'll want to continue to make notes after each practice session of daily meditation. Keeping a log of what took place during your meditation is another way of synthesizing your experience and making it a part of your daily life. You might notice temperature changes in your body; some people have even reported seeing lights or hearing sounds. You might go into a very deep silent space, or find your mind highly active. Sometimes a solution to a problem will arise spontaneously without your even focusing on it.

Often, people new to meditation will report that nothing happened, but "I noticed the headache I had was gone," "The pain I had in my back is gone," or "I just feel very peaceful." To the last statement, when asked, "Do you usually feel peaceful?" Invariably, the answer is no. So feeling peaceful is not something to be overlooked. This is another reason for making notes, so you can look back and see how your experience of meditation has changed and developed. Make a note of which exercises work best for you.

Once you complete the four-week program you can use any of the meditations in this book, including any of the inner focus techniques and mini-meditations, as your daily meditation.

Beginning the Process

Meditation is a learning process. It's a way in which we become more aware of ourselves and the outside world. As we heighten our consciousness through meditation, we become more in tune with ourselves and others. The more we find the peace and stillness within by meditating, the more we experience this same energy in our daily lives.

This feeling of peace builds up, and although you may not always be aware of the peace fund you've created inside, as you continue to practice you will find that it's always there for you.

Guidelines

Each day's meditation is preceded by a phrase which gives you the essence of the meditation. Read through the instructions for that day at least once to set them in your mind.

Before you begin, make sure that you're comfortable in whatever posture you've chosen and remember to use the three-part breathing technique. These preparations will make it easier to get into a meditative state.

The Four-Week Program

<u>WEEK ONE</u>
15 minutes

During your first week you'll be practicing for fifteen minutes every day. All of the different techniques are focuses that draw your awareness inside. Remember, the goal of meditation is to go *beyond* or *under* your thoughts so that you can rest in your inner silence.

Some of the meditations given here are similar to the focusing techniques elsewhere in the book. Having practiced them earlier, it will be much easier to recognize the thought-free state and to rest in it longer.

If your mind becomes active anytime during meditation, just watch it as you would a movie. Don't get involved in the thoughts, merely watch as they stream by, then return your attention to the focusing technique for that meditation.

At the end of the week, on the seventh day, check your log entries for the week and select the meditation that worked best for you. Repeat this exercise, adding five minutes to your practice time.

❦ DAY ONE

Counting as you breathe focuses the mind, allowing meditation to take place.

Sitting comfortably, close your eyes and focus on your breath. Taking long, even breaths through the nostrils, very slowly inhale the number one. Just as slowly exhale the number two. Slowly and evenly inhale the number three, and slowly and evenly exhale the number four. Continue breathing this way, in and out to the count of four with your mind focused on the numbers, for the remainder of the meditation.

If thoughts arise, return your attention to the breath.

❦ DAY TWO

Following a sound until it fades into nothingness silences the mind.

Sitting comfortably with your eyes closed, take a few deep breaths to center yourself. Using a bell, a gong, cymbals, or a pot cover, ring or strike it so that the tone resonates clearly. With the eyes closed, follow the sound until it slowly fades into nothingness. Stay with that nothingness for as long as possible. That nothingness is meditation. Repeat this exercise five times. The last time rest in meditation.

If thoughts arise, either witness them or repeat the tone.

❦ DAY THREE

Smelling your favorite fragrance releases a feeling of bliss.

Sitting comfortably, smell your favorite fragrance: a cologne, perfume, flower, incense, baby oil, soap. As you slowly inhale the fragrance, feel the joy arising from within. Now close your eyes and focus on the space from which that joy arises and let your mind rest there. The space from which the joy arises is the space of meditation. Repeat this three times, then rest in the space of meditation.

If thoughts arise, focus your attention on the fragrance once again or witness your thoughts.

❦ DAY FOUR

Focusing the awareness on one object brings the mind to a point of meditation.

Sitting comfortably and keeping your eyes open, take a few deep breaths to center yourself. Using a candle, a crystal, or a single flower, focus all your awareness on that one object until your mind merges with the object. The point at which nothing else exists is the point of meditation. Let your eyes close when they feel like it and continue to rest quietly in that inner space.

If thoughts arise, return your focus to the object.

❦ DAY FIVE

Focusing on a happy experience brings you to the source of your happiness. The source of your happiness is meditation.

Sitting comfortably with your eyes closed, recall an experience in which you were totally elated: your wedding day, the birth of a baby, graduation, getting a promotion. In your mind recreate all the details of the experience. Remember that feeling of happiness inside and let it dance in you again. Now find the place from which the happiness arises and rest there. This is the space of meditation. Relax in this space.

If thoughts arise, return to that happiness inside or just witness your thoughts.

❦ DAY SIX

Focusing on a colored form brings your mind to a still point. This point is meditation.

Sitting comfortably, take a few deep breaths to center yourself. Close your eyes and visualize *one* of the following colors—red, orange, yellow, pink, green, blue, or violet—in the form of a circle, triangle, or square. Keep focused on the color form until it disappears. The point at which the colored form disappears is the point of meditation. Rest in this space for ten minutes.

If thoughts arise, you can either watch them or return to the colored form and again focus on it until it disappears, then rest in that space.

❦ DAY SEVEN

Repeat one of this week's exercises that you felt was particularly powerful for you and add an additional five minutes.

Compare your journal entry from this exercise to your journal entry for your first experience of the exercise.

WEEK TWO
20 minutes

Some of the meditations presented this week are more subtle versions of the first week's meditations; you will recognize others as variations of inner focus techniques. These will feel like old friends to you, making it easier to sit for twenty minutes of meditation.

We've also included a waking meditation to help you remain aligned with your inner meditative energy while performing chores. This is an important practice as it teaches you how to connect to that energy no matter where you are or what you're doing.

Remember to keep making journal entries as you try each new meditation. On the seventh day, read through the week's entries and select the meditation you liked best. Use it as the meditation for that day by adding five minutes of practice time.

❦ DAY ONE

Following the breath as it comes in and goes out stills the mind.

Sitting comfortably with eyes closed, slowly inhale, breathing through the nose. Follow the breath as it comes in, breathing it into the heart region. Follow the breath as it goes out, slowly exhaling, letting the breath dissolve in the region of the heart.

Continue to follow the breath in this way. Any time thoughts arise, bring your awareness back to the breath.

❦ DAY TWO

**Following outer sounds until they fade into nothing-
ness brings you to the sound of your own inner silence.**

Sitting comfortably with your eyes closed, become aware
of the different sounds in the environment. Focus your
attention on each sound as you become aware of it and
follow that sound until it dissolves. As it dissolves let it
bring you into the silence that follows. That moment of
silence is meditation. Continue listening to the different
sounds surrounding you until you become unaware of any
sound, then just rest in silence.

If thoughts arise, witness them or return to focusing on
outside sounds.

❦ DAY THREE

Keeping the mind completely focused on whatever action you perform silences the mind and brings you to a state of inner peace and joy.

This is an exercise that will bring you to that space of meditation while performing actions in the waking state. Select a simple chore, such as cutting vegetables, washing dishes, polishing furniture, brass, or silver, cleaning the car, gardening—one that leaves your mind free. Focus all of your attention on the chore at hand. Be totally at one with whatever it is you are doing. Don't let your mind wander to something else that needs to be done.

Do the chore with love, as though whatever you are working on is the most precious of gems. Notice the surface becoming brighter and shinier, feel the textures, see the colors and forms, smell the smells, watch your hands as they work. Take your time with this exercise. When you find thoughts arising, mentally name whatever you are doing: washing, washing, washing, wetting the sponge, polishing, polishing. Keep repeating the name of the action you're performing to stay focused.

This exercise should be done for a minimum of twenty minutes, or for as long as your chore lasts. It should be done in silence; no music or TV in the background.

This exercise can be used at any time and will enrich your experience of daily tasks. Try to approach at least one task a day in this way and see how rich the moments we throw away can become.

✾ DAY FOUR

Creating your own innerscape brings you to an ideal place of rest deep within. This rest is meditation.

Sitting comfortably with your eyes closed, take a few deep breaths to center yourself. In your mind's eye, create your ideal place of relaxation. If it's the ocean, see the sun glinting on the waves as they roll onto the shore one after another. If it's the woods, hear the gentle breeze blowing through the trees, rustling the leaves. If it's a place that doesn't exist on earth, a place created purely in your mind, see all the details of this place in vivid color. Whatever your place of relaxation, see it in as much detail as possible. Know that this is your special place, one where nobody can disturb you. Incorporate any outside sounds into your innerscape and stay in this space for the remainder of the meditation.

❦ DAY FIVE

Dissolving each thought as it arises brings you to the place of meditation.

Sitting comfortably, take a few deep breaths to center yourself. Close your eyes and see yourself sitting in front of a fire. Watch closely as the flames dance before you. Each time a thought arises, silently offer it to the fire, mentally repeating, "I offer this thought about . . . to the fire." Let it dissolve in the flames. Watch as the thought disappears.

The space where the thought dissolves is the space of meditation. Stay there as long as possible. When the next thought arises, offer that thought to the fire and watch it as it disappears. Continue this practice for the rest of the meditation, trying to expand the thought-free state each time.

❦ DAY SIX

**Focusing on a heart-shaped object with your aware-
ness on the heart region brings you to your place of
inner love. This place is meditation.**

Sitting comfortably with your eyes closed, take a few
deep breaths to center yourself. Visualize either a pink or
green heart-shaped gem over the region of your heart. Focus your awareness on this radiant gem and feel its rays of
love bringing warmth to the heart region, gradually filling
every cell of your being with that love.

If thoughts arise, return your focus to the heart-shaped
gem, or just witness the thoughts.

✾ DAY SEVEN

Repeat one of this week's exercises that you felt was particularly powerful for you and add an additional five minutes.

Compare your journal entry from this exercise to your journal entry for your first experience of the exercise.

WEEK THREE

25 minutes

This week you'll be spending twenty-five minutes a day in meditation. A few of the meditations this week are more subtle versions of those you're already familiar with. The more subtle the focus, the less active the mind tends to be, allowing you to travel to deeper realms.

One of the surprises awaiting you this week is meditation on a mandala, a circular design that draws your focus into the center of the design and at the same time, to your own center.

Remember to follow the sequence given for the week, then choose your favorite for Day Seven, adding another five minutes to your practice time.

❦ DAY ONE

Focusing the attention on the space between breaths brings the mind to a point of stillness.

Sitting comfortably with your eyes closed, inhale to a count of five, pause for a count of one, then exhale to a count of five. Continue for at least ten repitions, then rest in the silence of the inner space for the remainder of the twenty-five minute meditation.

If thoughts arise, return your attention to inhaling to the count of five, pausing for the count of one, and exhaling to the count of five.

❦ DAY TWO

Inhaling and exhaling the syllables I AM brings you to a place of meditation.

Sitting comfortably, close your eyes and take a few deep breaths to center yourself. Mentally repeat the syllables I AM on the inhale, I AM on the exhale. Taking a long deep breath through the nose, breath in I AM. Exhaling slowly through the nose, breath out I AM.

Keep repeating I AM until the words disappear. If thoughts arise, witness the thoughts or return to repeating I AM.

❦ DAY THREE

Mandalas have the power to draw your awareness inward and take you into meditation.

Sitting comfortably, take a few deep breaths to center yourself. With your eyes open, look at the mandala pictured below. As you gaze at it, remember to breathe slowly and evenly in and out.

Focus all of your awareness on the mandala. Center your attention in the middle of the mandala, yet remain aware of the entire image. Let the mandala draw your awareness into it. Do this for a minute or two. Now, with your eyes closed, visualize the mandala. Let it draw your attention inward . . . inward . . . inward . . . until it disappears.

If thoughts arise, drop them into the center of the mandala.

❦ DAY FOUR

Visualizing an object brings the mind to a point of meditation.

On Day Four of the first week, you focused on an object (a crystal, a candle). This time you are going to visualize that same object. Sitting comfortably with your eyes closed, take a few deep breaths to center yourself. See the object in your mind. Recreate all of the details of that object. If it was a flower, notice the color and the shape of the petals. Recall everything you can about it.

If you visualize a crystal, see all of the facets of the crystal, remember how it caught the light, perhaps capturing a rainbow inside.

If you visualize a candle, watch the movement of the flame as you see it in your mind. See the blueness at the base of the flame and watch the candle closely as it flickers.

Focus on the object until it dissolves, then rest in the space where the object dissolves.

If thoughts come up, offer them to the flame or watch them disappear into the crystal.

Compare your journal entry from this experience to your first experience of this exercise.

🍏 DAY FIVE

Focusing the awareness on a point of light between the eyes guides you to a point beyond the light. This point is meditation.

Sitting comfortably with your eyes closed, take a few deep breaths to center yourself. Visualize a small white light between your eyes. Focus all of your awareness on this point of light, just above the bridge of the nose.

If thoughts come up, let them go and return your awareness to the white light. Remain focused on the light until it disappears, then rest in this space.

❦ DAY SIX

Letting the consciousness expand beyond the body takes you to the place of bliss.

Sitting comfortably, take a few deep breaths to center yourself. Close your eyes and focus on feeling your consciousness inside your body. Become aware of that energy within you. Now feel yourself slowly expanding a foot beyond your body in all directions. Expand your consciousness to fill the room you are in. Now feel yourself expanding beyond the walls of the room until eventually, you fill the entire building. Very slowly, feel yourself expanding to include the street you live on, then the entire block, then the whole town, village, or city, then the state you live in, then the country you live in, and then the planet. Now expand your consciousness to include all the planets, and then the stars and galaxies. Imagine that you encompass the entire universe.

Take lots of time with this exercise. Set your timer for twenty-five minutes, but if you take longer, that's okay, too. If you finish the exercise before the timer goes off, rest in this state of expanded consciousness for the remaining time.

❦ DAY SEVEN

Repeat one of this week's exercises which you felt was particularly powerful for you and add five minutes.

Compare your journal entry from this experience to your first experience with the exercise.

<u>WEEK FOUR</u>
30 minutes

This week will stretch your meditation practice to a half hour a day. If you should find you're feeling any physical discomfort as a result of sitting for thirty minutes, it's okay to quietly shift your position. You can draw your knees up, keeping your feet flat on the floor or stretch your legs out in front of you.

Each one of the meditations this week will take you still deeper inside, as you watch the focus of the day dissolve into silence. When thoughts arise, gently dissolve them into the focus of the exercise. Use your journal entries to help you recognize the different stages and levels you reach each day.

On the seventh day, add five minutes to your favorite meditation of the week.

❦ DAY ONE

Coordinating syllables with the incoming and outgoing breath takes you to a place deep within. This is the place of meditation.

Sitting comfortably, take a breath or two to center yourself. You will be repeating the sounds mmmm and shhh silently to yourself as you inhale and exhale. Close your eyes and inhale deeply through the nose, breathing in mmmm, exhale through the nose, breathing out shhh. Inhale mmmm. Exhale shhh.

The place where the sounds dissolve is the place of meditation. If thoughts arise, return to inhaling mmmm and exhaling shhh.

❦ DAY TWO

Focusing on the sounds within lets you experience your inner stillness.

Sitting comfortably with your eyes closed, take a few deep breaths to center yourself. Listen to the sounds of silence inside. Go deeper. Listen to the sounds from a place deep within. Let those sounds take you deeper and deeper into meditation.

Rest in this silence for the remainder of the meditation. If thoughts arise, let them go and return your attention to the inner sounds.

❦ DAY THREE

Letting your thoughts flow with a river takes you to a place of meditation.

Sitting comfortably, take a few deep breaths to center yourself. Close your eyes and imagine yourself sitting on the banks of a river. Watch the river as it flows by. Watch the water as it rolls past you downstream. Focus all of your attention on the flowing water. Watch the ripples on the surface of the water. Be one with the river.

If thoughts arise, place them in the river and watch the current carry them away. Let the river take all of your thoughts as you drift into a place of meditation. Rest in that space for the remainder of the meditation.

❦ DAY FOUR

Letting your consciousness dissolve into a blue sky lets you experience your inner bliss.

Sitting comfortably, take a few deep breaths to center yourself. Close your eyes and imagine a vast blue sky, the color you see on the most glorious spring day or summer afternoon. Feel the lightness of the sky, the vast expanse of blue stretching out to the horizon. You might even be able to see a few billowy white clouds in the distance. Watch the clouds as they slowly dissolve into the blue sky.

If you become aware of thoughts, let them dissolve in that vast blue sky in the same way the clouds do.

Feel that light and airy expanse of blue inside. Remain focused on the blue sky until it disappears. Rest in that space for the remainder of the meditation.

❦ DAY FIVE

Focusing your awareness on the fading sunset takes you deep into the velvet blackness beyond.

Sitting comfortably, take a few deep breaths to center yourself, then close your eyes. Imagine a sunset in its last brilliant moment, just before nightfall. Visualize a thin streak or band of bright crimson or orange light against a black velvet sky.

Focus all of your attention on the color. As night descends, watch the color as it slowly fades, dissolving into the rich black sky. Let the fading color carry you into the peaceful darkness of the night sky.

If thoughts arise, watch them fade into the night sky. Meditate on the velvet blackness surrounding you.

❦ DAY SIX

Awareness of the radiant light within fills us with a lightness of being.

Sitting comfortably, take a few deep breaths to center yourself. Keeping the spine straight, close your eyes and visualize a golden light originating at the base of your spine. Feel this light radiate its warmth as it slowly ascends the spine. Feel the light as it moves up through the lower back, then into the chest, and finally up through the neck to the head. Now feel the light filling the head, surrounding it with a golden glow. Feel this light filling your whole body until it radiates this golden glow.

Rest in this golden glow. If thoughts arise, return to the golden light and follow it as it moves slowly up the spine.

❧ DAY SEVEN

Repeat one of this week's exercises which you felt was particularly powerful for you and do it for an extra ten minutes.

Compare your journal entry from this experience to your first experience with the exercise.

A Final Word

Now that you've reached the end of your month-long program, remember, this is only the beginning. This is the perfect time for you to go over your journal entries and all of the written exercises you completed throughout the course of this book. You may notice that your perceptions and outlook on life have already expanded somewhat, allowing you to embrace life more fully. The more you meditate and contemplate the whys and hows of your life, the fuller your life will become, making each day a new adventure.

For this reason, we recommend an hour of meditation every day. You can build up to an hour using increments of five or ten minutes a week—whatever seems comfortable and practical for you. You may find that you want to meditate twice a day—half an hour in the morning and a half hour at night. Or you may prefer a full hour in the morning or evening. This all depends on your nature and your lifestyle. Length of practice is very individual.

If you find you don't have the hour on a particular day, but you can spare fifteen minutes, go for the fifteen minutes. Even five minutes is better than nothing. It's important not to push yourself. You don't want to make meditation a chore, you want it to be a place of peace. What is important is that you meditate every day. Once you become established in daily meditation, you'll find that you feel so much better when you do it that you'll make whatever effort it takes to find the time.

You can use any of the inner focuses or mini-meditations in this book as your daily meditations. As we said earlier, you'll find that some techniques will appeal to you more than others. Review your journal entries to find the ones that work best for you. You can change your meditation each day or continue with a particular favorite. The point is not *how* you reach the meditative state, but getting there.

Keep in mind that meditation is not a static practice, it changes, grows, and evolves over time, as you do. As you continue to meditate, you may want to read through the exercises every so often and try some new ones. You'll discover that you'll have different favorites at different times.

You may want to begin or end your daily meditation with some hatha yoga postures. This will help ease any physical discomfort you may experience after sitting in one position for an hour. There are many books available on hatha yoga as well as many classes taught throughout the country.

You may also want to share meditation with friends and family and get together once a week for a group meditation. This not only deepens your connection to the inner self, it deepens your connection with others.

If you have found that you want to become more deeply involved in meditation, we suggest you call SYDA Foundation at 914-434-2000 for a list of Siddha Meditation Centers in your area. We recommend Siddha Meditation because of our own experience on this path and because it is headed by one of the greatest living masters of meditation in modern times, Gurumayi Chidvilasananda. In her presence meditation is spontaneous and effortless, and people experience great love and ecstasy as they soar to new realms of inner and outer discovery.

It is our hope that you will continue on the path of meditation. You have the key, the door is unlocked, and the adventures are limitless.

Joy be with you!

Bibliography

Arguelles, Jose and Miriam. *Mandala*. Shambhala Publications, Inc., Boston and London, 1972.

Belhayes, Iris with Enid. *Spirit Guides*. ACS Publications, Inc., San Diego, 1985.

Benson, Herbert with Miriam Z. Klipper. *The Relaxation Response*. William Morrow and Company, Inc., New York, 1975.
——— and Joan Z. Borysenko. "The Relaxation Response and Relaxation Techniques." *Mind/Body/Health Digest*, Vol. 2, No. 2, New York, 1988.

Bukkyo, Dendo Kyokai. *The Teaching of Buddha*. Buddhist Promoting Foundation, Tokyo, 1966.

Campbell, Joseph and Bill Moyers. *The Power of Myth*. Doubleday, New York, 1988.

Capra, Fritjof. *The Tao of Physics*. Shambhala Publications, Inc., Boston and London, 1983.

Chidvilasananda, Gurumayi. *Kindle My Heart*. Prentice Hall Press, New York, 1990.

Clark, William. "The Unhealthy Sound of Victory." *Discover*, May 1988.

Foundation for Inner Peace. *A Course in Miracles*. Foundation for Inner Peace, 1975, 1985.

Gelman, David and Mary Hager. "Body and Soul." *Newsweek*, November 7, 1988.

Goleman, Daniel. "Why Do People Crave the Experience?" *New York Times*, August 2, 1988.
———. "Hypertension? Relax." *New York Times Magazine*, December 11, 1988.
———. "Agreeableness vs. Anger." *New York Times Magazine*, April 16, 1989.

————. "Researchers Find That Optimism Helps the Body's Defense System." *New York Times,* April 20, 1989.

Greeley, Andrew. *Ecstasy: A Way of Knowing.* Prentice-Hall, Englewood Cliffs, NJ, 1974.

Horn. J. C. "Dome-inating the Game." *Psychology Today,* October 1988.

Jenny, Dr. Hans. "The Sculpture of Vibrations." *UNESCO Courier,* December 1969.

Johari, Harish. *Chakras: Energy Centers of Transformation.* Destiny Books, Roshester, Vermont, 1987.

Maslow, Abraham. *Toward a Psychology of Being.* D. Van Nostrand Company, New York, 1968.

Muktananda, Swami. *Meditate.* SYDA Foundation, South Fallsburg, New York, 1980.

————. *I Have Become Alive.* SYDA Foundation, South Fallsburg, New York, 1985.

————. *Where Are You Going?* SYDA Foundation, South Fallsburg, New York, 1981.

Peale, Norman Vincent. *The Power of Positive Thinking.* Foundation for Christian Living, Pawling, New York, 1978, 1952.

Perls, Dr. Frederick S. *Gestalt Therapy Verbatim.* Real People Press, Moab, Utah, 1969.

Ram Dass. *Grist for the Mill.* The Unity Press, 1976.

Reps, Paul. *Zen Flesh, Zen Bones: A Collection of Zen Writings.* The Charles E. Tuttle Company, Rutland, Vermont, and Tokyo, Japan.

Shainberg, Lawrence. "Finding 'The Zone.' " *New York Times Magazine,* April 9, 1989.

Sheinkin, David. *Path of the Kabbalah.* Paragon House Publishers, New York, 1986.

Siegel, Bernie S. *Love, Medicine, and Miracles.* Harper & Row, New York, 1986.

Silva, Jose. *The Silva Mind Control Method.* Pocket Books, New York, 1977.

Singh, Jaideva. *Vijnanabhairava or Divine Consciousness.* Motilal Banarsidass, New Delhi, India, 1979.

Zukor, Gary. *The Dancing Wu Li Masters: An Overview of the New Physics.* Bantam, New York, 1984.